LEISU
PEAK
AND DI

CW00555683

EXCELLENT BOOKS

EXCELLENT BOOKS
94 BRADFORD ROAD
WAKEFIELD
WEST YORKSHIRE WF1 2AE
TEL: 01924-315147
e-mail: richard@excellentbooks.co.uk

First Published 1997
First Reprint 2001
Second Reprint 2002

ISBN 1 901464 01 6

Whilst the author has cycled and researched all the routes for the purposes of this guide, no responsibility can be accepted for any unforeseen circumstances encountered whilst following them. The publisher would, however, welcome any information regarding any material changes and any problems encountered.

Front and rear cover photos: Macclesfield Forest

Printed by

CARNMOR PRINT

95/97, London Road, PRESTON, Lancs. PR1 4BA
Tel: 01772 555615 Fax: 01772 555615 E-mail: carnmorprint@aol.com

PEAK DISTRICT AND DERBYSHIRE FAMILY AND LEISURE CYCLE RIDES

PAGE

INTRODUCTION

EXCITING NEW DAYS OUT FOR THE WHOLE FAMILY

There is a glut of guides for cyclists to the Peak District but very few concentrate on routes specifically for families and leisure riders. The criteria used within these pages are, however, simple; as much use as possible is made of specially constructed cycle tracks, well-surfaced bridleways and quiet minor roads, thus avoiding, to a large extent, heavy traffic. All the circular rides are of moderate length. Attractions suitable for families are also pointed out, so a simple bike ride is turned into a fun day out. Planning your day out is made easy with information on access, eating places and a host of other practical advice.

THE LANDSCAPE

The Peak District National Park covers much of the upland mass bounded by Sheffield, Chesterfield, Derby, Leek and Manchester. Also being within easy reach of the Leeds/Bradford conurbation and Birmingham it attracts huge numbers of visitors; you may see annual visitor figures of 20 to 30 million bandied about!

It is traditionally divided into two very contrasting geographical areas, the Dark Peak, based on gritstone, and the White Peak, reflecting the light colour of the limestone rock that is preponderant in the southern area. The main northern mass of the Dark Peak is contained in the boggy, flat fells of Kinder Scout and Bleaklow Hill, whilst two prongs at its edges project southwards. The westerly prong is delineated by Axe Edge and the famous rocks known as the Roaches. The easterly prong contains prominent lines of cliffs such as Stanage Edge. Dark Peak areas above 2000ft (660m) may often be found shrouded in mist; indeed 20 inches more rainfall may be registered on the Dark Peak plateaus in contrast to the lower altitudes of the White Peak. The White Peak has a less menacing feel; green rolling hills are broken by spectacular white cliffs, caverns and 'dales', many more precipitous than their broad based counterparts in the Yorkshire Dales National Park.

To the south the hills run out towards Derbyshire and the land becomes flatter. The Peak's major southern rivers unite to eventually join the river Trent. Hereabouts the landscape is less spectacular but plenty of interesting villages, stately homes and pastoral solitude await the visitor.

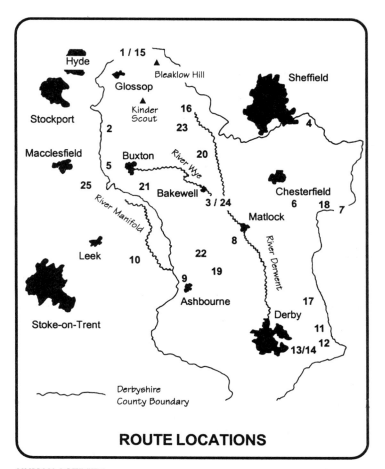

ROUTE LOCATIONS

HUMAN ACTIVITY

Dark Peak land is hard to farm and sheep farmers in this area are a special breed. Forestry is commercially viable and very much in evidence in such areas as Derwent Reservoir (ride 16). The heather on the very tops is also an ideal habitat for the grouse, cultivated commercially for shooting. Greater evidence of more intensive agricultural activity is apparent in the White Peak as, in some areas, numerous dry stone walls divide the land into tiny parcels.

A great variety of mining has historically been present throughout the area. Limestone quarrying, providing aggregate for road foundations, is arguably the biggest blot on the landscape, especially notable around the Castleton area. Its proponents, of course, point out that it is one of the major employers in the area. As well as the more mundane lead, fantastically coloured minerals were extracted from a number of sites around Castleton.

Railways came and went leaving a legacy of ready prepared trails ideal for cyclists such as the High Peak and Tissington Trails. More permanent reminders of man's influence are reservoirs such as the vast expanses of Howden, Derwent and Ladybower, supplying places as far apart as Sheffield and Leicester with drinking water.

CYCLING WITH CHILDREN AND BEGINNERS' TIPS

The following summary is obviously a generalisation when it comes to what a child is able to do at a certain age and is only a guide to what you should be considering for your child(ren). Under the age of six most kids don't have sufficient balance and coordination to ride unaided and are normally carried or pulled by an adult in one way or another; explore the possibilities of child seats (mounted behind or in front of your seat), trailers and trailer bike attachments.

a. **Front Seats** are generally considered suitable for shorter distances. Fitting onto the crossbar, the child is cradled by the rider's arms. A bike with an upright riding position (mountain bike, city bike or hybrid) is essential as their geometry allows you to control the extra central weight. Suitable for 9 months to 3 years, they will carry 15kg/33lbs. Generally, no harness is supplied so they are not considered as safe as other types of child carriers.

b. **Rear Seats** will take slightly more weight (22kg/48lbs) and have a harness. Rigid, moulded plastic is the standard material and you should also ensure your model has a safety harness and footrests to stop the child's legs becoming caught in the wheel. Do not use in conjunction with a sprung saddle - fingers can get caught in saddle springs. A headrest is also useful. Suitable for ages 9 months to 5 years. Front and rear seats start at about £30.

c. **Trailers**, attaching to a seatpost or chainstay, will carry two young children (or a handy load of shopping!), but obviously mean hillier routes will be difficult. Remember to fit a rear offside light when travelling on the road. Reputable brands start at around £250.

d. **Trailer cycles** turn a normal bike into a tandem, allowing a child between 5 and 10 to accompany you. The trailer cycle does not have front forks or a wheel, so it can attach to the rear of your bike, allowing the child to help with pedalling only. From £200 up.

e. Tandems (those suitable for children are known as juniorbacks) are suitable for ages four to ten years old. Alternatively 'kiddy-cranks' may be fitted to a normal tandem. Tandems are expensive, starting around £400, but the Tandem Club (25 Hendred Way, Abingdon, Oxfordshire OX14 2AN 01235 525161) may be able to put you onto a cheaper second hand buy through their magazine.

General points to bear in mind when carrying children by bike are:

* Carrying a child adds quite a lot of weight so it is doubly important your bike is well maintained, stable and easy to control with good brakes.
* Extra gears are also useful given the extra weight.
* You have more momentum so allow longer to stop.
* If carrying a child on a rear seat balance the weight by putting some weight in front 'low rider' panniers.
* All child passengers should wear a helmet.
* Never leave a child sitting on a bike / in a trailer unattended.

FAMILY GROUP ON THE MONSAL TRAIL

At ten many children are able to ride confidently and are able to be taught the essentials of road sense (obviously absolutely vital, even on the quietest minor roads). A list of important pointers is shown below but a **recognised cycling proficiency course is strongly recommended** before your child even sets out on the road.

* Ride on the left, about 1 metre out from the kerb. Riding close to the road edge only encourages other vehicles to squeeze past you making accidents more likely.
* Always signal and never make unpredictable movements. This is especially true of potholes - 'stand' off your seat and go straight over them unless you are absolutely sure there is no traffic behind.
* Adopt the correct position at junctions - if a junction looks difficult get off and walk.
* Ride behind your child so that traffic coming from behind sees you, the largest obstacle, first and slows down sufficiently quickly.

EQUIPMENT AND TECHNIQUE

Clearly the most important piece of equipment is a bike that you can ride comfortably and safely. Some routes in this guide are really only suitable for mountain bikes, or at the very least the less common hybrid 'all terrain bikes'. Some of the circular rides follow minor roads and are suitable for racers and many of the specially constructed trails can also be used by racers (see the 'Length and Difficulty' section for an idea of what to expect). You should know how to do basic maintenance and carry the following basic tools suitable for the jobs described:

Kit	Fault
Puncture repair kit and spare inner tubes with air pump;	Bust inner tubes.
Tyre levers;	" " "
Range of spanners;	Changing of wheels if not quick release. Other common adjustments e.g. if pedal becomes loose.
Small screwdriver;	Adjusting gear mechanisms.
Adjustable spanner;	Will fit a number of nuts on the bike if they work loose.
Allen keys to fit various adjustments;	Handlebar stem, seat post etc.

Chainsplitter;	This tool not only takes chains apart but you <u>may</u> be able to rejoin your chain if it breaks whilst riding. Spare links are also useful for rejoining.
Pliers;	Tightening brake and gear cables.
Small change and friend's phone number;	For when you are utterly stuck because of mechanical failure of bike/car!

N.B. There are special bike 'combination tools' that contain a number of the above tools and save a lot of weight e.g. Cooltool or Ritchey combination tool.

Keep moving parts, especially the chain and rear mechanism, well lubricated and free of dirt. For a complete guide to maintenance see Haynes 'The Bike Book'. A helmet should always be worn (conforming to one of the usual safety standards) and thrown away after an impact. I find the other most useful clothes items to be;

* Padded shorts or three quarter length bottoms depending on the weather. Special cycling shorts help to prevent saddle soreness.
* Durable footwear with a chunky sole to grip the pedal. Some pedal systems have clips or the facility to 'screw' the underneath of a sole to the pedal which can be useful to keep your feet on the pedals over rough ground. Practise disengaging your feet quickly from the system so you can use it safely.

* Good waterproof, breathable tops and bottoms.

* Waterproof cycling gloves. (Fingerless ones are very useful in warmer weather).

You heat up quickly on a bike so you should have the capability to take off and add a couple of layers of clothing and keep dry spares in panniers or a small backpack. Too much weight or too large a backpack will destabilise you.

High energy foods such as bananas and nuts are excellent - chocolate only raises your blood sugar levels for a short while then leaves you feeling even more tired than before. Try to snack and drink water often rather than breaking once for a big meal; this way there is an even supply of energy to your body. A water bottle is therefore very useful. A solid lock will enable you to leave your bike and explore nearby attractions only accessible on foot e.g. Thor's Cave.

NAVIGATION

Map and compass are vital pieces of safety equipment. If you follow the directions in the book accurately (and presuming the features used as direction finders are not altered) you shouldn't have any problems. However, should you become lost these two aids are the key to finding your way back home quickly and safely. There are plenty of guides on safety in the mountains which give you accurate instructions on map reading and other important techniques. Bike computers can help in giving determining distances and average speed along with a wealth of other statistics of your journey. The higher up you go, the further from a main settlement or phonebox and the harsher the weather conditions, the more potentially vital will become your map reading technique. Its importance cannot be stressed enough. Please bear this advice in mind, even for these leisure rides of modest length and difficulty.

THE MOUNTAIN BIKE CODE OF CONDUCT.
(With the author's own additions in italics)

RIGHTS OF WAY

* Bridleways - open to cyclists but you must give way to walkers and horse riders. *(Legally, they should be signposted at junctions with public roads but this isn't always the case. Also note horses, especially young nervous ones, can be very scared of bikes. When they are coming in the opposite direction it's best to stop. When you approach from behind give a gentle 'excuse me' if you think the riders haven't heard you. If you scare a horse it can bolt causing injury to the rider or those nearby).*

* Byways - Usually unsurfaced tracks open to cyclists. As well as walkers and cyclists you may meet occasional vehicles which also have a right of access.

* Public footpaths - no right to cycle exists.

Look out for posts from the highway or waymarking arrows (blue for bridleways, red for byways and yellow for footpaths).

NB The above rights do not apply in Scotland.

OTHER ACCESS

* Open land - on most upland, moorland and farmland cyclists normally have no right of access without the express permission of the landowner.

* Towpaths - a British Waterways cycling permit is required for cyclists wishing to use their canal towpaths. **(Do not allow children unsupervised on canal towpaths - they are unguarded).**

* Pavements - cycling is not permitted on pavements.

* Designated cycle paths - look out for designated cycle paths or bicycle routes which may be found in urban areas, on forestry commission land, disused railway lines or other open spaces.

* Cyclists must adhere to the Highway Code.

FOLLOW THE COUNTRY CODE.

* Enjoy the countryside and respect its life and work.

* Guard against all risk of fire.

* Fasten all gates.

* Keep dogs under close control.

* Keep to rights of way across farmland.

* Use gates and stiles to cross fences, hedges and walls.

* Leave livestock, crops and machinery alone.

* Take your litter home.

* Help to keep all water clean.

* Protect wildlife, plants and trees.

* Take special care of country roads.

* Make no unnecessary noise.

SAFETY

* Ensure that your bike is safe to ride and prepared for all emergencies.

* You are required by law to display working lights after dark (front and rear).

* Always carry some form of identification.

* Always tell someone where you are going.

* Learn to apply the basic principles of first aid.

* Reflective materials on your clothes or bike can save your life *(obviously this applies doubly to road sections)*.

* For safety on mountains refer to the British Mountaineering Council publication " Safety on Mountains ."

* Ride under control when going downhill since this is often when serious accidents occur.

* If you intend to ride fast off road it is advisable to wear a helmet.*(I recommend it on all routes at all times)*.

* Particular care should be taken on unstable or wet surfaces.

RIGHTS OF WAY.

Although the legal position is set out in the code of conduct above the situation on the ground may not be that simple. There are many minor roads shown on maps but their status is not clear from the map alone and may need further research. Bridleways may be shown on a map but may not exist when you look for them or may be obstructed when you try to ride along them. Similarly many rights of way that exist for bikes may not be shown on the map.

These problems are solved by this guide; all routes were fully legal at the time of going to press and their legality has been researched extensively by the author. However, it is still strongly recommended to take the appropriate map and a compass in case you do happen to become lost. The Pathfinder maps are the most detailed showing features such as individual fields. More useful for the Peak District are the two Outdoor Leisure maps (no's 1 and 24, Dark Peak and White Peak areas). Landrangers show less detail but give greater coverage. My own directions and maps will complement the OS maps whilst sometimes giving detail as to rights of way not recorded on the OS maps.

KEY TO DIRECTIONS

Annotations;
R = right, turn or bear right
L = left, turn or bear left

USEFUL ADDRESSES

Cyclists Touring Club, Cotterell House, 69 Meadrow, Godalming, Surrey GU7 3HS 01483 - 417217

British Cycling Federation, National Cycling Centre, Stuart Street. Manchester M11 4DQ 0161 2232244

Peak Camping Barns. Phone 01200 420102 for information on basic 'stone tent' accommodation throughout the Peak District.

The National Trust, High Peak Estate Office, Edale End, Edale Road, Hope 01433 670368. It is particularly useful to be a member as there are some fine properties in Derbyshire, for example Calke Abbey (see route 13), to which membership gives you free access.

Information Offices

Bakewell 01629 816316
Castleton, Castle Street (near Parish church) 01433 620679
Edale (Between railway station and village) 01433 670207
Fairholmes (Derwent Valley, between Ladybower and Derwent Reservoirs) 01433 650953
Langsett Barn 01226 370770
Glossop 01457 855920
Derby (Assembly Rooms, Market Place) 01332 255802
Buxton 01298 25106
Ashbourne 01335 343666
Chesterfield 01246 345777
Matlock Bath 01629 55082
Burton upon Trent 01283 516609

MOUNTAIN RESCUE

Dial 999 and tell the operator the required service. Give the number of the phone and stay there until the emergency services ring you back. Make sure you give your location as accurately as possible.

1. LONGENDALE TRAIL

LENGTH AND DIFFICULTY *A return trip along the whole of the trail is about 21km / 13 miles.*

MAPS *OS Outdoor Leisure 1, Dark Peak Area. Landranger 110, Sheffield and Huddersfield.*

TIME ESTIMATE *3 hours.*

FACILITIES

Information *There is a good information centre in Glossop 01457 855920.*

Eating *There is sometimes a snack van at Torside car park and there are plenty of opportunities in Hadfield.*

BIKE ACCESS POINTS

Torside car park, off the B6105, north east of Hadfield, or the car park near Hadfield station are good starting points.

ALONG THE WAY

*The Longendale Trail itself lies on the line of a dismantled railway that once ran through **Woodhead Tunnel**. You can get a look at the latter by following the Longendale Trail west as you emerge onto it from the car park. **Woodhead Chapel** has links with the tunnel for it is here that many navvies who died whilst constructing the Woodhead Tunnel are buried. You can see some of their graves here. The poor condition of the church over the centuries reflects the fact the upper valley was scarcely populated apart from two 'booms' caused by the growth of the cotton industry and secondly by the building of the dams and the railway tunnel.*

*The Trail is part of the **Trans-Pennine Trail**, which is still being constructed in many other places. The target date for completion is 2000 but the route is already about 58% complete (70% for walkers). Eventually it will link Southport to Hull, mainly using disused railways, canal towpaths, riverside towpaths and existing rights of way. It will link to European long distance routes by using the ferry from Hull but it will also effectively form an English coast to coast route.*

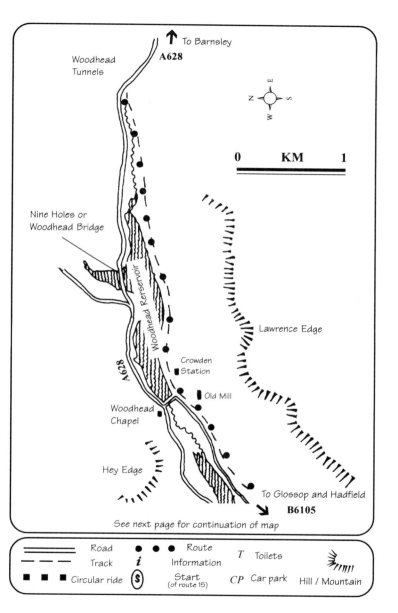

To Barnsley
A628

Woodhead Tunnels

Nine Holes or Woodhead Bridge

Woodhead Rerservoir

Lawrence Edge

A628

Crowden Station

Old Mill

Woodhead Chapel

Hey Edge

To Glossop and Hadfield
B6105

See next page for continuation of map

═══ Road	● ● ● Route	T Toilets		
- - - Track	*i* Information			
■ ■ ■ Circular ride	(S) Start (of route 15)	CP Car park	Hill / Mountain	

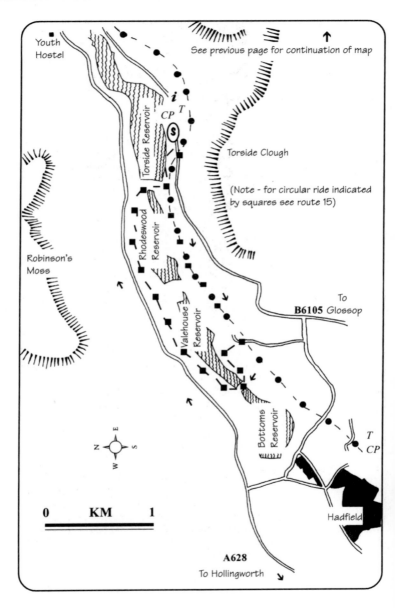

Youth Hostel

See previous page for continuation of map

Torside Reservoir

i

CP *T*

Ⓢ

Torside Clough

(Note - for circular ride indicated by squares see route 15)

Rhodeswood Reservoir

Robinson's Moss

Valehouse Reservoir

To
B6105 Glossop

Bottoms Reservoir

T
CP

N
E
W
S

Hadfield

0   KM   1

A628
To Hollingworth

16

2. SETT VALLEY TRAIL

LENGTH AND DIFFICULTY *4km / 2.5 miles (8km / 5 miles out and back). Very flat, short and easy. Ideal for younger children (but several roads must be crossed). The Kinder Road extension 3km / 1.9 miles (6km / 3.8 miles out and back) is harder, with some small gradients and can be busy with weekend traffic up to the car park.*

MAPS *OS Outdoor Leisure 1, Dark Peak. Landranger 119, Sheffield and Huddersfield.*

TIME ESTIMATE *3-4 hours for both the trail and the Kinder Road extension.*

FACILITIES

Cycle Hire and Information *At the start of the trail in Hayfield (the former Hayfield station). Open Easter. From then on Saturday and Sunday, 9 until 6, until the 14th June, when it opens every day for the summer season. Also open May Bank Holiday and school half term week (late May). Phone 01663 746222. Information centre also at Torr Top (not accessible by bike).*

Eating *Picnic sites near the start and at Wilde's Crossing and a cafe at Birch Vale.*

BIKE ACCESS POINTS

Hayfield *From the former train station. (Well signposted from the A624 and A6015 through Hayfield). This is the best start point.*
Birch Vale *Bridleway access from this village on the A6015*
High Hill Rd *Bridleway access from the A6015 just northeast of New Mills*
St. George's *Hidebank area of New Mills*
NOTE - West of St. George's Rd, approaching New Mills, the trail should not be used by cyclists.

Most of the Kinder Road extension is on public road. From Hayfield information centre cross the A624 dual carriageway and bear **R** to pass the church on your left. Cross over the bridge and go **R** down Bank St. just by the Old Bank Surgery. Soon bear **R** onto Kinder Rd. Climb on the road and continue on this road past the Sportsman Inn and Bowden Bridge car park on the left. Follow the road to in front of Kinder treatment works and bear **R** (marked a footpath but in fact a bridleway). Continue climbing through Farlands and climb on this track until meeting a 'private' sign.

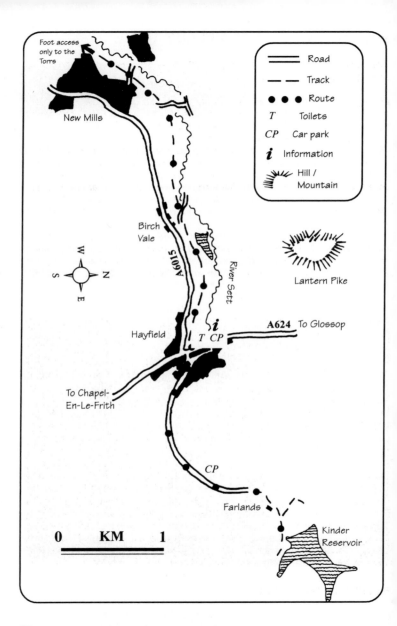

Foot access only to the Torrs

New Mills

Birch Vale

A6015

River Sett

Hayfield

i Information

T CP

A624 To Glossop

Lantern Pike

To Chapel-En-Le-Frith

CP

Farlands

Kinder Reservoir

	Road
	Track
● ● ●	Route
T	Toilets
CP	Car park
i	Information
	Hill / Mountain

N W S E

0   KM   1

ALONG THE WAY

*The trail follows the route of the **Hayfield Railway line** opened in 1868 whose primary function was to serve the mills built along the Sett Valley. Coal and raw materials were brought up the valley and finished products taken away. Calico printing was a major industry here in the nineteenth century. Many villagers also travelled from the valley to Manchester. It was such a popular weekend trip, in fact, that up to 5,000 passengers could use the line on a Sunday in the 1920's. Local industrial decline also spelt the death of the line which closed in 1970. Despite the semi-urban setting the leafy trail houses a number of bird species. Looking over the reservoir at Birch Vale there is a good view of the side of Lantern Pike. By locking up your bikes at St. George's Rd. you can continue on the trail on foot to the Torrs, a spectacular natural gorge at the confluence of the rivers Goyt and Sett. There are leaflets available on the Torrs Industrial Heritage Trail and the Torrs Riverside Bridges Trail from the information centre here.*

*On the **Kinder Road extension** look out for the plaque in the car park marking the **1932 mass trespass** on Kinder Scout. Great views of the western edge of Kinder Scout (a huge plateau at the centre of the Dark Peak which tops 2,000 ft.) await you.*

THE SETT VALLEY TRAIL (ROUTE 2)

3. MONSAL TRAIL

LENGTH AND DIFFICULTY *11.2 km / 7 miles for a return trip along the whole trail. Ideal family cycling; a former railway line means gradients are negligible and there are interesting features at both ends of the trail. A return journey to Monsal Head is about 12km (7miles) and to Rowsley and back is about 10km (6 miles). Some road cycling is required to reach Monsal Head on a 'B' road suitable only for the more confident rider. There is a good track to Rowsley, undulating and rocky in places, which can be picked up at the eastern end of the trail although some short sections may have to be pushed.*

MAPS *OS Outdoor Leisure 24, The White Peak. Landranger 119, Buxton and Matlock.*

TIME ESTIMATE *The trail is little more than 1 hour's ride return trip. Add on another one to two hours for either a trip to Monsal Head or Rowsley.*

FACILITIES

Cycle Hire *Bike Active, Bakewell Station 01629 814004. 1st April - 30th September, 10 am to dusk. 1st October - 31st March, weekends, school holidays, Bank Holidays and by prior arrangement.*

Information *Bakewell Tourist Information Centre 01629 813227*

Eating *The Countryside Bookstore has a drinks machine and the Stable pub and tearoom is at Monsal Head. Cauldwell's Mill at Rowsley has a tearoom and of course there are all facilities in Bakewell.*

BIKE ACCESS POINTS

Hassop; old station car park
Bakewell; old station car park - probably the most convenient start point
Coombs viaduct; from minor road / track to Coombs farm from Bakewell.

If going on to Rowsley come off the trail at Coombs Road viaduct and carry on under the disused railway. Pass Coombs Farm and at the next major junction of tracks (4 meet at the same point) head straight across. From thereon stay on the track, avoiding left turns up to Lees Moor Wood, into Rowsley.

Note there is no exit at the northwestern end of the trail. The final exit is at the former station near Thornbridge Hall, which will take you onto the road for Monsal Head.

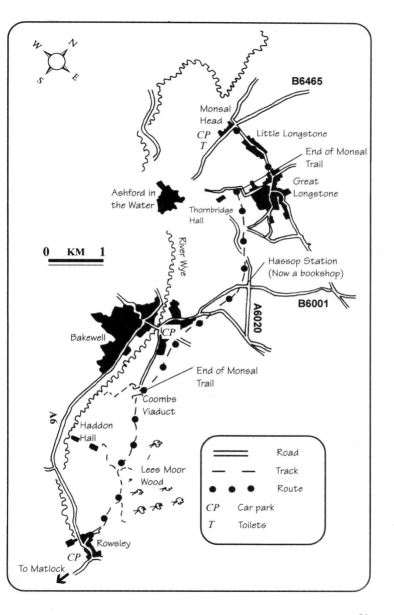

ALONG THE WAY

As it is based on a stretch of the former London to Manchester railway, the section of the trail open to cyclists passes through two interesting former stations. **Bakewell station** was constructed for the Duke of Rutland only after the railway company building the line had assuaged his fears over its course. He was concerned about the effect of the line on his section of the Wye Valley and was only persuaded to consent by the building of a tunnel behind Haddon Hall. The Duke of Devonshire blocked the progress of the line further up the Derwent than Rowsley and even negotiated a private station for himself named after nearby **Hassop**. This is now the Countryside Bookstore and warehouse. Bakewell station was closed in 1967. On the small spur down to Coombs viaduct there are good views over the Wye Valley. The trail itself ends at Haddon Tunnel which has been sealed off due to its dangerous condition. The attractive market town of **Bakewell** is associated with 'tarts', more properly named puddings which are available at several shops.

The beautiful **Haddon Hall** is just to the southeast of Bakewell off the A6, a product of numerous phases of building from the 12th to the 17th centuries. It is still owned by the Duke of Rutland, having belonged to his ancestors for over 800 years. It has superb terraced gardens and its incredible ambiance have made it the set for such films as 'Jane Eyre' and 'The Princess Bride'. Daily 11am - 5pm, late March until the end of September. Licensed restaurant. Admission charge. Telephone 01629 812855.

The cycle section of the trail terminates at Monsal and gives a superb view of **Monsal Viaduct.** Its construction was opposed by conservationists but today it blends with the landscape and is considered an attractive feature of the Upper Wye Valley. Trains ran on the line between Buxton and Matlock and then onto London which received thousands of churns of milk brought down the Wye Valley on the line.

The charming village of **Rowsley** is a short ride from Coombs Rd. viaduct. The Peacock Hotel was once Rowsley Hall and bears the crest of the Manners family, a peacock. **Cauldwell's Mill**, a nineteenth century sawmill, cornmill and fulling mill, has been restored to working condition and its water turbines can be seen in operation grinding to make flour which is sold on the premises. It has a teashop and the Grouse and Claret pub also offers refreshment nearby. Open 1st March - 31st Oct every day (10am - 6pm from 1st April) and 1st November - end of February, weekends only (10am - 4.30pm). Admission to mill: Adults £2, children and OAPs £1.

4. ROTHER VALLEY

LENGTH AND DIFFICULTY *Rother Valley Country Park - Staveley (Beighton-Staveley trail) is about 20km / 12.4 miles return journey. It is 34km / 21.2 miles from Rother Valley to Chesterfield, return journey.* **Note the Chesterfield Canal section was not being publicised as a cycling route** *at the time of writing as it contains a number of road crossings because of low bridges. These crossings will eventually be avoided. This means it is not up to the high standard which will eventually be the norm on the Trans-Pennine Trail, of which it is part. However multiuser surface has been laid most of the way meaning it can be cycled. There are no significant gradients. Rother Valley Country park itself has several kilometres of off road bike tracks within its own grounds.*

MAPS *OS Landrangers 119 and 120, Mansfield / Worksop and Buxton /Matlock.*

TIME ESTIMATE *4-5 hours to Chesterfield and back. To Staveley and back will take 2-3 hours and takes in some very pleasant scenery.*

FACILITIES

Cycle Hire and Information *Both are found at Rother Valley Country Park. If the Visitor Information Centre doesn't have sufficient information try the Rangers' Office across the courtyard. Cycle Hire from the watersports centre on 0114 2471453. Opening times vary depending on daylight hours so please phone first. Chesterfield Tourist Information is at 01246 345777.*

Eating *There is a cafe near the visitor centre at the country park and plenty of cafes and pubs if you make it to Chesterfield centre. As the trail crosses the B6050 on the edge of Brimington there is The Mill pub.*

BIKE ACCESS POINTS

There are numerous access points which can be gleaned by looking at an OS map but the best way onto the trail, especially for children, is at **Rother Valley Country Park***. From the main car park (accessed off the A618 to the east of the country park) follow the edge of the main lake to round its northern end and onto the far side. About halfway down the lakeside and just after passing through a gate bear* **R** *under a railway bridge. The wide track of the Beighton-Staveley trail is on your* **L***.*

The only difficulty with navigation comes at Staveley when changing over from the Beighton Staveley track onto the Chesterfield Canal; at the edge of Staveley you bear **R** approaching the railway line and cross over it on the road bridge

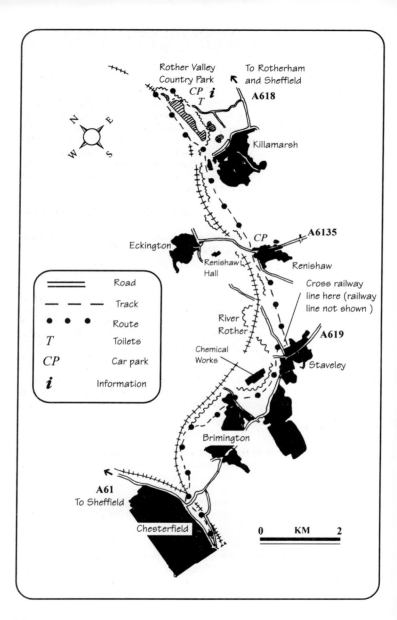

(**carry required here down steps** bearing **R** at the bottom of the steps). Head on the track towards the large works with the spiral looking tower and across a road, following the Trans-PennineTtrail badge. You pick up the canal side in a short while and follow it to Tapton Lock at Chesterfield.

ALONG THE WAY

Rother Valley Country Park *is a pleasant collection of lakes amidst grassy landscape with a variety of sporting activities and things to see. 18 and 9 hole golf courses and driving ranges are complemented by canoe and dinghy hire and cable water skiing. The visitor centre is based around a mill that has been restored and is open to visitors at certain times of the year.*

The **Beighton to Staveley Trail** *runs along a former railway line that served this predominantly coal-producing area. However, much of the trail has been recolonised by wildlife and it is an excellent opportunity to observe the green, agricultural landscape of the area. The trail and canal sections will eventually form a spur of the* **Trans-Pennine Trail.**

Renishaw Hall *is near the trail. Its gardens and museums were the home of the local Sitwell nobles for nearly 400 years. Open Easter-September 10.30 am - 4.30 pm.*

The Chesterfield Canal *was built in the 1770s and connected Chesterfield to the Trent, allowing bulk movement of coal and iron and giving access to the Humber. The canal is currently undergoing a restoration programme which aims to make it navigable along its whole length. It also doubles as a long distance footpath, the Cuckoo Way, named after Cuckoo barges that used to operate on the canal. They were 70 feet long and only a few feet wide and could take up to 27 tonnes of cargo.* **Chesterfield** *is most famous for the* **crooked spire** *of its parish church and also has a fine market square (market days Monday, Friday, Saturday).*

THE FAMOUS CROOKED SPIRE AT CHESTERFIELD (ROUTE 4)

5. GOYT VALLEY

LENGTH AND DIFFICULTY *12 km / 7.4 miles for a return journey. The main road section climbs next to the river for nearly its whole length. Great on the long downhill run but meaning some stamina is required in the opposite direction. The Hoo Moor track extension is somewhat flatter but a climb up the valley is required to get to it.* **This is not a dedicated cycle trail but mainly public road. It is, however, suitable for car free cycling on Sundays and bank holidays (10.30 am to 5.30 pm) from the start of May to the end of September. During these times it is closed to most motor traffic but be aware of walkers and wheelchair users. At other times it is a normal one way road and not suitable for family cycling.** *From the Derbyshire Bridge car park a tricky compact stone track climbs over the corner of Axe Edge Moor to Buxton for a couple of kilometres.*

MAPS *OS Outdoor Leisure 24, White Peak. Landranger 119, Buxton and Matlock.*

TIME ESTIMATE *A couple of hours should give you plenty of time to explore the valley by bike.*

FACILITIES

Cycle Hire *None in the Goyt Valley itself.*

Information *The nearest tourist information office is at Buxton 01298 25106 but there are several information boards at the Goyt Valley car parks.*

BIKE ACCESS POINTS *Start from the car parks at either The Street or Derbyshire Bridge.*

ALONG THE WAY

This area was once famed for its natural, wild beauty and its remoteness. The building of **Erwood Hall** *and quarrying and coal mining in the nineteenth century went some way to ending this isolation. There is a footpath (no bike access) to the site of Erwood Hall which was demolished in the 1930s and the remains of a gritstone quarry can be seen further south, higher up the valley. The greatest changes came in the twentieth century when Stockport Corporation built Fernilee and Erwood Reservoirs (1938 and 1967) and the Forestry Commission started planting here in 1963. There are also many popular walks in the area to unusual natural features such as Shining Tor and Axe Edge.*

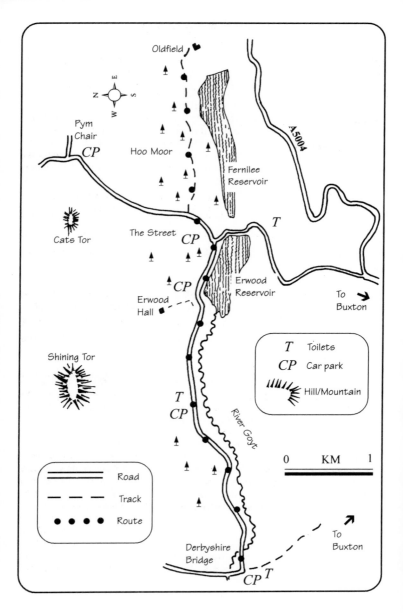

6. FIVE PITS TRAIL

LENGTH AND DIFFICULTY *12km / 7.5 miles on a circular ride starting in and returning to Tibshelf. There are only a small number of moderate inclines on this mainly flat trail. You will briefly encounter some urban traffic as the trail passes through Holmewood.*

MAPS *OS Landranger 120, Mansfield and Worksop.*

TIME ESTIMATE *1-2 hours.*

FACILITIES

Information *There is no information centre nearby. Contact the Ranger Service at 23 Market Street, Clay Cross 01246 866960 for further details.*

Eating *There are several picnic sites along the trail plus cafes in Tibshelf and Holmewood centres.*

BIKE ACCESS POINTS

At numerous places in and around Tibshelf, Pilsley and Holmewood, some signposted and others not. The trail is often waymarked for walkers with yellow arrows. There are also useful destination signposts along the trail. See the map for car park access.

ALONG THE WAY

*Despite being former coal mining country the countryside around the Five Pits is rapidly returning to nature, as former derelict land has become a site for newly established plants, ponds and meadows. As the name suggests the site is based on five former coal pits and the rail lines that served them; coal production ceased in 1973. Other areas of the reclaimed land have been used for agriculture and industry. Some remains of the old industry remain such as the pithead buildings of Williamthorpe Colliery, visible on the trail north of Holmewood. The most famous local landmark, the 228 feet **twisted spire** of St. Mary and All Saints Church in Chesterfield, is about 4 miles from the trail (see route 5 for details). **Hardwick Hall** has its own circular route (see route 18) which can be reached from Timber Lane Car Park through Astwith.*

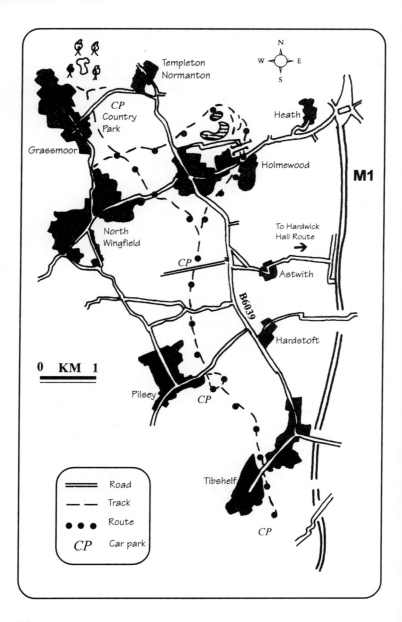

7. PLEASLEY TRAILS NETWORK

LENGTH AND DIFFICULTY *There are approximately 15km (9 miles) of trails suitable for bikes in the network. Use the map to plan your own route, **but note the Rowthorne Trail is for walkers only.** The tracks are usually good and flat but beware of some steepish gradients, especially when coming off the trail onto roads.*

MAPS *OS Landranger 120, Mansfield and Worksop.*

TIME ESTIMATE *You should be able to cover most of the tracks in 2-3 hours easily.*

FACILITIES

Cycle Hire and Information *At Teversal Trail visitor centre 01623 442021.*

Eating *There are pubs in Pleasley and in Fackley, near Teversal.*

BIKE ACCESS POINTS

Common Lane, east of Pleasley
At several places in Pleasley
Batley Lane (easterly branch of Teversal trail only)
Skegby South of Skegby on the B6028 (Stoneyford Lane)
Teversal (near the Teversal Trail visitor centre)

ALONG THE WAY

*The trails used are based on former railway lines that served the pits in this traditional coal mining area. There were pits at Teversal, Pleasley and Silverhill and the impressive **Pleasley Mills**, spinners of yarn, required their own rail sidings for the supply of raw materials. Three mills remain standing today, although they have been converted to industrial units. In **Pleasley Village** are the remains of a steam house that was attached to a now demolished corn mill. Steam power was used when there was an insufficient head of water to power the mill (much water was taken out of the river by factories further upstream).*

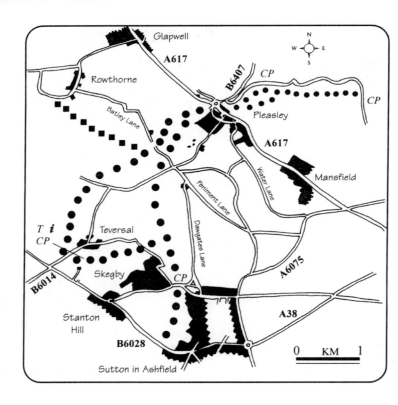

	Road	■ ■ ■ ■ ■	Rowthorne Trail (no cyclists)
● ● ● ● ●	Teversal Trail	CP	Car park
		T	Toilets
● ● ● ● ●	Meden Trail	i	Information office

Note-trails are colour coded along the way

8. HIGH PEAK TRAIL

LENGTH AND DIFFICULTY *28km / 17.5 miles. Most of the trail is flat, as you would expect of a former railway line. However, there is a 4km section from High Peak Junction to Middleton Top Visitor Centre dominated by steep, lengthy inclines **only suitable for very fit and experienced riders***. *This difficult section can be used as a link onto the Cromford Canal (cycling not publicised but allowed).*

MAPS *OS Outdoor Leisure 24, The White Peak. Landranger 119, Buxton and Matlock.*

TIME ESTIMATE *The whole trail is full day's ride (a good 6-7 hours). The 'Along the Way' notes will help you pick a section or devise your own circular ride.*

FACILITIES

Cycle Hire *Cycle Hire centres at Middleton Top and Parsley Hay on the trail. Parsley Hay opens every day except Christmas 01298 84493. Middleton Top has a complicated pattern of seasonal opening, best confirmed by phone 01629 823204.*

Eating *You can pick up limited snacks at the information centres and there may be some farmhouse tearooms open on the way. You are best advised to take your own snacks, however, as you do not pass through any major settlements. Worksworth, Middleton, Carsington, Brassington and Pomeroy, off the trail, have either pubs or cafes.*

BIKE ACCESS POINTS *Best accessed at the car parks or as shown on the map.*

ALONG THE WAY

This is a mainly flat track through limestone pasture, but see the note above about the difficult section that includes Sheep Pasture and Middleton inclines. It is worth taking a lock to be able to lock your bikes up and explore nearby features on foot. This way you can explore short sections of the trail one at a time and see its most interesting features close up. The best scenery is between Middleton Top and Minninglow. Travelling east to west the main features adjacent to the trail are;

High Peak Junction *Here are the remnants of former railway buildings with*

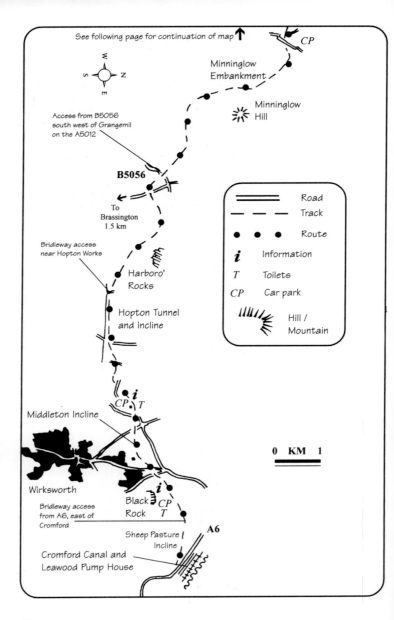

See following page for continuation of map ↑

CP

Minninglow
Embankment

Minninglow
Hill

W
N
S
E

Access from B5056
south west of Grangemil
on the A5012

B5056

To
Brassington
1.5 km

Bridleway access
near Hopton Works

Harboro'
Rocks

Hopton Tunnel
and Incline

	Road
– – –	Track
● ● ●	Route
i	Information
T	Toilets
CP	Car park
⎧⎭⎫	Hill / Mountain

i
CP   T

Middleton Incline

0   KM   1

Wirksworth

Bridleway access
from A6, east of
Cromford

i
Black   CP
Rock   T

Sheep Pasture
Incline

A6

Cromford Canal and
Leawood Pump House

34

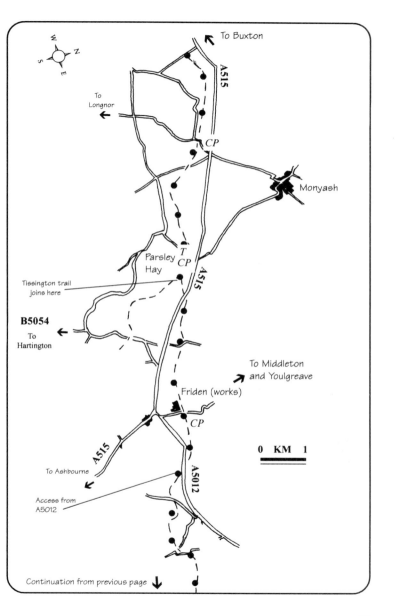

To Buxton

A515

To Longnor

CP

Monyash

Parsley Hay

T
CP

A515

Tissington trail joins here

B5054

To Hartington

To Middleton and Youlgreave

Friden (works)

CP

A515

To Ashbourne

Access from A5012

A5012

Continuation from previous page ↓

the former railway workshop now acting as a visitor centre. Before ascending the incline to the engine house note the catchpit at the bottom. It was built to prevent a repeat of the incident when two wagons ran back down the incline and gathered so much speed they cleared the canal and railway line and ended up in a field. **(Note - extreme gradient here - only for experienced riders).**

Sheep Pasture Engine House No engine remains, simply a shell. Once used to haul wagons up the 1,320 yard incline.

Black Rocks The eponymous rocks are a local beauty spot and climbers' paradise. They can be accessed from the trail by foot only.

Wirksworth Nowadays an attractively restored market town it was once the centre of the Derbyshire Lead Mining Industry. The Wirksworth Heritage Centre is housed in the old silk and velvet mill whilst the **National Stone Centre** is an exciting exploration of geology right next to the trail (open all year). St. Mary's church can only be approached on foot and contains unusual features such as carvings in a sarcophagus lid from AD 800 set into the wall and an unusual presbytery.

Middleton Top Engine House Now a visitor centre it also houses the 1829 steam engine that pulled wagons up the Middleton Incline. There are usually several demonstrations of the engine from March through to April.

Hopton Incline Preceded by an unlit tunnel, trains had to use their own power to get up here, which made it the steepest gradient worked by locomotives in the British Isles.

Harborough Rocks Objects ranging from Paleolithic to medieval times have been removed from the large cave here. Still visible are stones shaped like a pulpit, chair and font. The summit triangulation point has terrific views. Foot access only.

Brassington has a good mix of 16th to 18th century architecture including the fine Olde Gate Inn with an enormous kitchen range in the bar.

The Royston Grange Trail is accessible on foot near Minninglow car park. It guides you through Bronze Age, Roman and Medieval periods.

HARBOROUGH ROCKS ON THE HIGH PEAK TRAIL (ROUTE 8)

9. TISSINGTON TRAIL

LENGTH AND DIFFICULTY *21km / 13 miles. There is a slight uphill gradient going away from Ashbourne but nothing that should trouble even beginners.*

MAPS *OS Outdoor Leisure 24, White Peak. Landranger 119, Buxton and Matlock.*

TIME ESTIMATE *About 4 hours to cover the whole trail and return.*

FACILITIES

Cycle Hire *In trail car parks at Ashbourne 01335 343156 and Parsley Hay 01298 84493.*

Information *At Ashbourne 01335 343666 and at Hartington signal box (alongside the trail).*

Eating *There numerous pubs and cafes at villages along the way including ones at Tissington (cafe - seasonal), Fenny Bentley (pub), Biggin (pub) and Hartington (pubs and cafes).*

BIKE ACCESS POINTS *As indicated on the map.*

ALONG THE WAY

Tissington *has been called the most beautiful village in England. It certainly presents an almost perfect picture-postcard scene, with its beautiful Jacobean hall, ancient church, old school and duck pond. Also look out for the former house of a blacksmith family, decorated with key, lock and horseshoe motifs.* **Fenny Bentley** *can only be reached by a busy section of main road but has a very unusual tomb at the Church of St. Edmund, King and Martyr. Effigies of a couple lie on top whilst their 21 offspring are depicted tied in bags around the side (possibly a 'get-out' by the sculptor who didn't have likenesses of the children to work from)!* **Hartington** *is yet another picturesque village. Its factory cheese shop, old hall, church and arched former town hall (now a shop) cluster around a compact centre. The information centre on the trail here is a beautifully restored signalling box.*

Dovedale *is rightly famed for its natural beauty. Its steep limestone sides house numerous unusual rock formations, many with quirky names such as the Twelve Apostles and Tissington Spires. It is accessible only on foot; approach by leaving the trail and passing through Thorpe, a charming limestone village. Leave your bike in the car park on the approach road. If you come on a sunny Sunday afternoon be prepared to share the dale with up to 4,000 other visitors!*

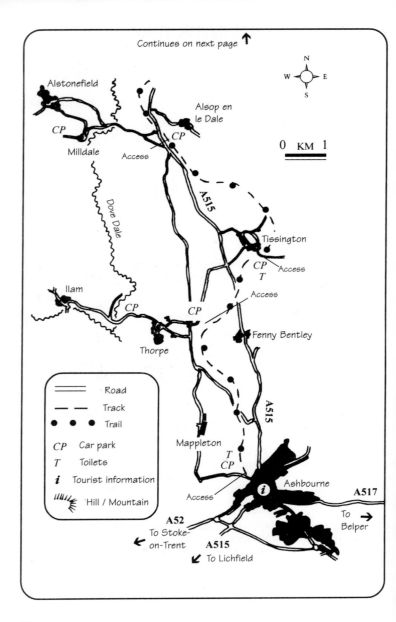

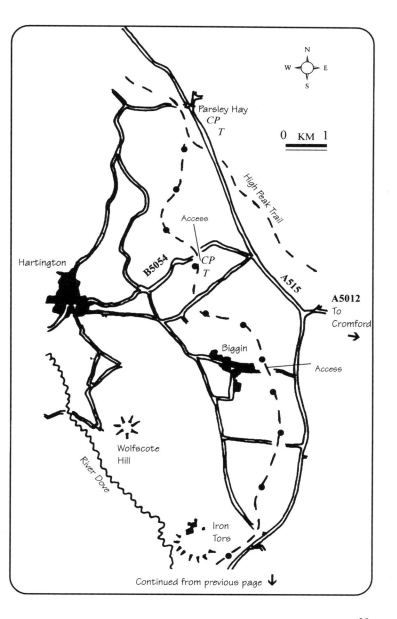

A WELL AT TISSINGTON (ROUTE 9)

10. MANIFOLD WAY

LENGTH AND DIFFICULTY *26km / 16 miles return trip. This is a very even tarmac path with only a very slight gradient uphill from Waterhouses to Hulme End. Its moderate length make it an ideal beginner's track. There is one short road section but a much quieter, alternative, gated road section is indicated on the map.*

TIME ESTIMATE *3 hours.*

MAPS *OS Outdoor Leisure Map 24, White Peak Area. Landranger 119 Buxton and Matlock.*

FACILITIES

Cycle Hire *Waterhouses, Old Station Car Park 01538 308609.*

Information *The nearest staffed information centre is at Ashbourne but there is an unmanned centre with information boards about the trail in the former station building at the Hulme End terminus of the track.*

Eating *There is a cafe at Wettonmill on the trail and pubs at Hulme End and Waterhouses. There are village pubs off the trail in Wetton, Grindon and Butterton (the last also has a craft centre serving teas).*

BIKE ACCESS POINTS

At the southern and northern ends of the trail (Waterhouses and Hulme End) Weag's Bridge
Wettonmill
Wetton Bridge

Pick up the alternative section (see 'Length and Difficulty) either near the tunnel at Swainsley, on the other side of the river, passing Swainsley Hall, signed for Wettonmill. If heading south-north, at Wettonmill bear left through farm buildings, keeping the river on your left.

ALONG THE WAY

*Like many other cycle trails the **Manifold** is based on an old railway line. 'A line that started and finished nowhere' was one assessment of the Leek and Manifold Light Railway (1904-34). This proved to be a just judgement as the railway, built to exploit copper mining at Ecton, but most of all the agricultural produce of the Peak area, soon began to flounder. The oversize wagons used on the line had specially made carriers made to sit on the narrow gauge railway whilst*

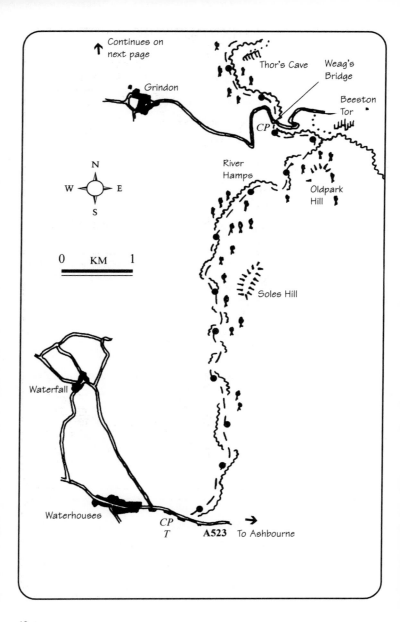

Continues on next page

Thor's Cave

Weag's Bridge

Beeston Tor

Grindon

CP

River Hamps

Oldpark Hill

N
W   E
S

Soles Hill

0   KM   1

Waterfall

Waterhouses

CP
T

A523   To Ashbourne

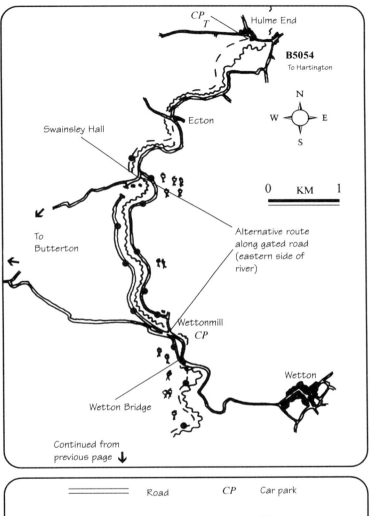

Map labels:

CP T — Hulme End

B5054 To Hartington

N W E S

Ecton

Swainsley Hall

0 KM 1

Alternative route along gated road (eastern side of river)

To Butterton

Wettonmill CP

Wetton

Wetton Bridge

Continued from previous page ↓

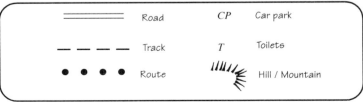

══════	Road	
– – – –	Track	
● ● ● ●	Route	
CP	Car park	
T	Toilets	
〰〰	Hill / Mountain	

the engines were based on designs intended for India! The only village stops were at either end with the eight intermediate stops being basic platforms. There was even a tourist stop at Thor's Cave (see below).

The most striking geographical landmark in the beautiful Manifold valley is **Thor's Cave.** This spectacular limestone outcrop can be explored on foot from the trail and is signed (steep path-can be muddy). It houses a gaping cave which it is thought was once used by prehistoric hunters (beware - cave entrance slippy) and gives fine views down the valley. Further south is **Beeston Tor**, also accessible on foot (you must bear left over the river at Weag's Bridge and then bear off right on foot to reach these impressive cliffs). The valley itself has been compared in its beauty with Dovedale but is often significantly quieter. The river Manifold dissapears at Wettonmill and follows an underground course to reappear in the grounds of Ilam Hall. The last two miles of the trail to Waterhouses follow the river Hamps. In early summer the riverbed is full of Butterburr or Wild Rhubarb (beware - poisonous). **Waterfall** is perhaps the prettiest village near the trail.

THE ALTERNATIVE SECTION TO THE EAST OF THE RIVER MANIFOLD (ROUTE 10)

11. LONG EATON TO HEANOR

LENGTH AND DIFFICULTY *A return trip to Straw Bridge from Long Eaton is around 18km / 11 miles. The flat path is well prepared and is very new in places. If you want to get to Shipley Country Park you will have to use a section of 'A' road from whatever direction you approach it. A suggested link is shown on the map. However, the trail is planned to be finished before April 1998 and this road link will not be necessary then, as the trail will run to Shipley Country Park. The latter has its own network of bridleways featured in route 17.*

MAPS *OS Landranger 129 Nottingham.*

TIME ESTIMATE *2-3 hours.*

FACILITIES

Cycle Hire *At Shipley Country Park (see route 17).*

Information *Although there is no tourist information as such in Long Eaton you can ring Leisure Services for information 0115 9461321. Cycle Wise, at 0115 9734176, is an organisation that promotes cycling in general and has lots of cycling information and free indoor lock-up facilities for bikes. It is found on Derby Road, opposite the council buildings, near the start of the trail.*

Eating *There are plenty of places in Long Eaton and Sandiacre but nothing really on the route itself (sometimes there is a snack van as you pass through the industrial area, just after joining the Nutbrook Canal branch of the trail). There is a cafe at Shipley Country Park (see route 17).*

BIKE ACCESS POINTS

As the trail is unfinished and has not yet reached Shipley Country Park it is best accessed from Long Eaton (see map for town centre access) or from the parking ground at Straw's Bridge lake on the A609 (Derby road) just to the west of Ilkeston. You can also get onto the trail at:

Long Eaton, off Bennet St, opposite Toton railway sidings
At Sandiacre off Station Rd (B5010)
Crompton Rd at Stanton Works industrial area

The trail is generally easy to follow but is not yet signed. If in doubt follow the navigational tips on page 47.

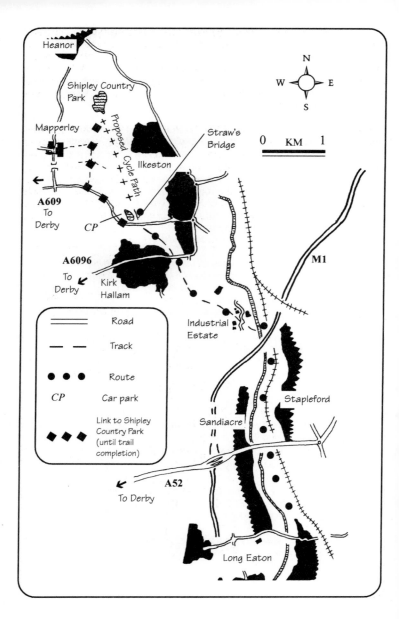

Heanor

Shipley Country Park

Mapperley

Proposed Cycle Path

Straw's Bridge

Ilkeston

N
W — E
S

0   KM   1

A609
To Derby

CP

A6096
To Derby

Kirk Hallam

M1

Industrial Estate

Stapleford

Sandiacre

A52
To Derby

Long Eaton

Road

Track

Route

CP   Car park

Link to Shipley Country Park (until trail completion)

a. TO JOIN NUTBROOK CANAL BRANCH After joining the trail in Long Eaton centre quickly come alongside the Erewash Canal. Follow the canal out of Sandiacre to pass under the M1 bridge and at the first lock after the bridge head **L** over the canal onto a well-made tarmac path (Nutbrook information board shortly on the right). Stay on the main track, passing through an industrial estate and ignoring any tracks joining, to continue to Straw's Bridge (just after passing under the A609).

b. LINK FROM STRAW'S BRIDGE TO SHIPLEY COUNTRY PARK (Pending completion of cycle path). Just after passing over Straw's Bridge you will see a lake down to the left with a parking ground and main road at the far side (down to the right is the back of a housing estate then a golf course - the track may have been built here by the time you read this). Bear **L** and pass the lake to meet the main road. Go **R** onto the road and uphill. Just past the Newdigate Arms pub go **R** down a small road which becomes a track. Follow the track, ignoring any splits off to the right and left. This will bring you into Shipley Country park on Slack Road (see map in route 17).

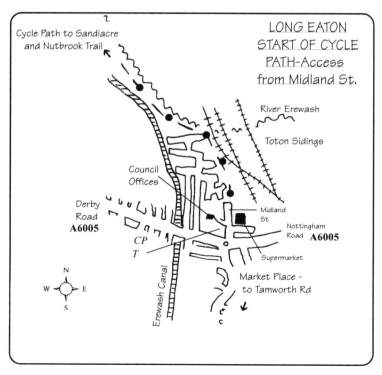

Cycle Path to Sandiacre and Nutbrook Trail

LONG EATON START OF CYCLE PATH-Access from Midland St.

River Erewash

Toton Sidings

Council Offices

Derby Road **A6005**

Midland St

Nottingham Road **A6005**

CP

T

Erewash Canal

Supermarket

Market Place - to Tamworth Rd

N
W — E
S

ALONG THE WAY

*The finely preserved **Erewash Canal** is followed for the first part of your journey. Although it weaves its way between the backs of houses and railway lines it still provides a charming, green, traffic-free ride. By 1962 it had become disused but has since been rescued from decline and neglect by an enthusiastic local group. The best example of their work is the lock cottage at Sandiacre, at the junction with the old Derby Canal. It is now the HQ of the canal preservation society (open Sundays throughout the summer). The canal was built in the late eighteenth century for Derbyshire and Nottinghamshire colliery owners who wanted to gain access to new markets. It was initially so successful that an original £100 share was worth £1,300 at one stage and in 1826 a 74% dividend was paid. Its decline was largely due to competition from the railways. Much less is left of the **Nutbrook Canal** which is followed for the latter part of the journey. Its 4.5 mile length was based on the coal and iron trades. Little of it now remains as much has been culverted or is overgrown. You can still see some of the original locks, for example at Straw's Bridge.*

EREWASH CANAL, NORTH OF LONG EATON (ROUTE 11)

12. TRENT AND MERSEY CANAL

LENGTH AND DIFFICULTY *Shardlow to Repton is 38km / 23.5 miles. - the good news is that the towpath is entirely flat. From Shardlow to Burton upon Trent is a lengthy 50 km / 31 miles or so. The whole canal length may be best explored in several visits. There is one road deviation from the path which avoids a walkers only section and which is slightly hilly and has a moderate level of traffic (a couple of kilometres only - therefore easily walkable). Of course, short lengths of the towpath are ideal for those wanting easy cycling but **do not leave children unsupervised - the canal has no barrier.** You do have to negotiate some busy town roads heading into Burton upon Trent from the canal so it may be best to lock up your bikes and walk.*

MAPS *OS Landrangers 128 and 129, Derby and Nottingham respectively.*

TIME ESTIMATE *The full 50 kilometres is a serious undertaking of at least 6 to 7 hours for more experienced riders only. Shardlow - Repton is a good 4 to 5 hours journey.*

FACILITIES

Information *Burton upon Trent 01283-516609.*

Eating *There are numerous pubs and cafes alongside or near the canal including establishments at Shardlow, Swarkestone Lock, Swarkestone, Willington and of course Burton upon Trent.*

BIKE ACCESS POINTS *At numerous points along the canal. Note there may be a diversion around the southern Derby ring road (still being constructed at the time of writing).*

Shardlow - off the A6 road as is crosses the canal.
Aston on Trent - via a bridleway that runs behind Aston Hospital and past Weston Grange.
Weston on Trent - turn left off the main road down King's Mill Lane.
Several minor road crossings between Swarkestone and Willington and Willington itself.
Burton upon Trent - although you pass under numerous bridges coming into Burton the best exit options from the canal are the path bridge opposite the green area of Shobnall Fields (the next bridge after Dallow Bridge) or the road bridge immediately before Shobnall Marina.

To get onto the road section you must exit onto the Derby-Melbourne cycle path. The next bridge after bridge 11 is a black iron bridge (Sarson's Bridge). Turn onto the cycle way, which this bridge carries, and cross back over the

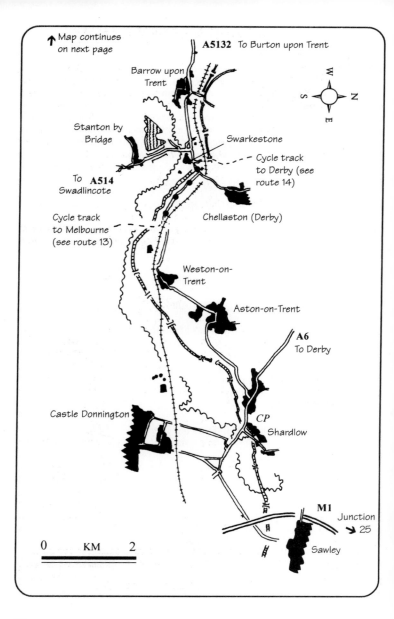

↑ Map continues on next page

A5132 To Burton upon Trent

Barrow upon Trent

Stanton by Bridge

Swarkestone

Cycle track to Derby (see route 14)

To **A514** Swadlincote

Cycle track to Melbourne (see route 13)

Chellaston (Derby)

Weston-on-Trent

Aston-on-Trent

A6 To Derby

Castle Donnington

CP

Shardlow

M1 Junction → 25

Sawley

0   KM   2

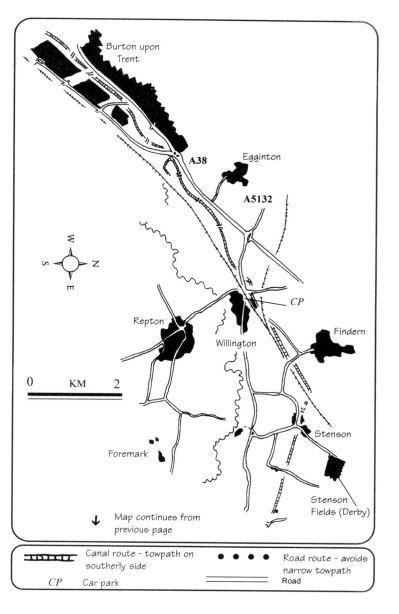

Burton upon Trent

A38

Egginton

A5132

CP

Repton

Willington

Findern

Foremark

Stenson

Stenson
Fields (Derby)

↓ Map continues from
previous page

⊥⊥⊥⊥⊥ Canal route - towpath on southerly side	•••• Road route - avoids narrow towpath
CP Car park	══ Road

canal on the bridge Follow the cycle path until it leads you to the road and bear **L** onto it. This slightly hilly and moderately busy road section brings you to a junction with the A514. Go **L** and immediately you cross over a bridge. Rejoin the canal path on the other side of the bridge and carry on towards Burton.

ALONG THE WAY

*The **Trent and Mersey Canal** was the brainchild of the famous potter, Josiah Wedgewood, and proved a great success when it opened in 1777, linking Liverpool and Hull. It carried huge amounts of china clay to potteries nearby the canal. Nowadays there is no trade but the canal has been preserved as a pleasure waterway and is protected by statute. The surrounding countryside is a pleasant flat or gently rolling green. **Shardlow** is a highly unusual village which has the Trent and Mersey Canal as its main street! There is a lot of well-preserved canalside architecture, the highlight being the eighteenth century Trent Mill. **Swarkestone's** best feature is its eighteenth century five arched bridge, found on the A514 south of the village. **Repton** is an outstanding historical town; see the map and key on page 53. **Burton upon Trent** is best known for its brewing industry which has bequeathed the town two museums - see map and key for details.*

THE REMAINS OF BAKEWELL STATION (ROUTE 3)

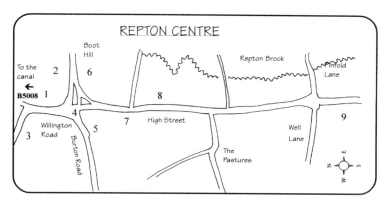

1. ST. WYSTAN'S CHURCH contains one of the oldest, intact buildings in England, the Anglo-Saxon crypt. King Ethelbald of Mercia was interred here in 757 AD (Repton was a principal residence of the Mercian royal family) and later King Wiglaf and St. Wystan. The crypt was later covered with floor boards and only discovered when a workman digging a grave fell into it.

2. PRIORY AND SCHOOL. The mid-13th century arch is all that is left of the priory gatehouse. You are allowed through the arch into the school yard as far as the east end of the crypt. From here you can see numerous buildings from various centuries; the Old Priory (12th), the ornate brick Hall (17th) dormers of the Old Priory (18th) and Pears School (19th).

3. The THATCHED COTTAGES date from the 17th and 18th centuries respectively.

4. The ANCIENT CROSS was at the centre of medieval markets. The hiring of farm workers and servants continued here well into the nineteenth century.

5. THE OLD MITRE was originally a boys' boarding house. It now houses Repton School staff.

6. THE POST OFFICE is a beautiful 18th century, Georgian brick building.

7. The OLD VILLAGE SCHOOL is now Repton School Department of Art.

8. The TUDOR LODGE dates from the late sixteenth or early seventeenth century. The timbers stand on stone that most probably came from the Priory.

9. NO.16 MAIN STREET is a strikingly grand residence built in 1703 for a former Lord Mayor of London.

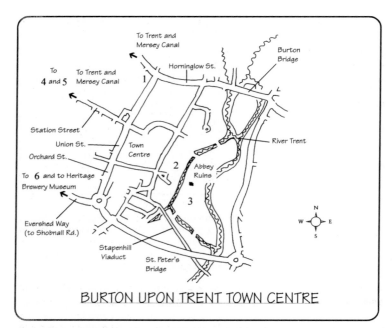

BURTON UPON TRENT TOWN CENTRE

1. The BASS MUSEUM is the most comprehensive museum on the history of brewing in the world. Attractions include old delivery vehicles and shire horses. The HERITAGE BREWERY MUSEUM (Anglesey Rd) has a similar theme.

2. The VICTORIAN MARKET is a splendid edifice and stands next to the Church of St. Modwen, rebuilt in 1719 and containing many interesting monuments to brewers!

3. ANDRESEY ISLAND is found in the green leafy Washlands Town park and is a great setting for a picnic. A chalybeate well (impregnated with iron) once attracted large numbers of pilgrims to it. The water tower here was built in 1856 to store water for brewing.

4. ST. PAUL'S SQUARE is a conservation area.

5. BOROUGH ROAD houses many fine buildings including Grain Warehouse No. 2. It still bears the crimson and cream paintwork of the Midland Railway Company.

6. SHOBNALL MARINA lies next to the canal. Pleasure cruisers can be hired .

13. ELVASTON CASTLE TO MELBOURNE

LENGTH AND DIFFICULTY *35km / 22 miles return trip to Melbourne Hall and 40km / 25 miles return trip to Calke Abbey (alternative routes marked on map). Although both trips are quite lengthy compared to others in the book, the majority of the rides are on specially prepared cycle path (beware some road crossings passing through Derby). There is some moderate road climbing to the south of the Trent. Melbourne Hall and Calke Abbey can be linked, to visit both in one trip, as suggested on the map, but you will have to negotiate some quite busy roads.*

MAPS *OS Landrangers 128 and 129, Derby and Nottingham.* **Note there is a large scale map of Elvaston Castle on page 61.**

TIME ESTIMATE *Four hours plus time to visit Melbourne Hall and / or Calke Abbey make this a full day's outing.*

FACILITIES

Information *Office at Elvaston Castle 01332 571342.*

Eating *Cafes at Elvaston Castle, Melbourne Hall Gardens and Calke Abbey plus several pubs in Melbourne and King's Newton.*

BIKE ACCESS POINTS *Elvaston Castle is the best place to access the route near Derby. For other access points see road crossings on the map.*

There are several points of difficulty in navigation, mainly because vandals have removed cycle way signs at crucial junctions. Directions below are given travelling from Elvaston Castle to Melbourne / Calke.

a. For directions from ELVASTON CASTLE onto the riverside path see the map on page 61.
b. ALVASTON PARK TO SWARKESTONE LOCK Pass the BMX track in Alvaston Park and at the edge of the park turn **L** by the lake, keeping it on your left. Take the next **R** to pass behind the large grey and brick building of Derby Tertiary College. Bear **L** at the next junction and go under London road about 50m after the junction. Continue on the cycle track out of Derby, through countryside to Swarkestone Lock (there is a small road section on Penalton Close).
c. SWARKESTONE LOCK-MELBOURNE Over the bridge by Swarkestone Lock turn **L** onto the canal tow path, keeping the canal on your left, following Melbourne signs. Just under the canal bridge the canal path is barred. Turn **R** onto the main road and immediate **R** over the bridge (signed for Weston and Aston). About 1km after this junction a sign directs you off the road, just before a

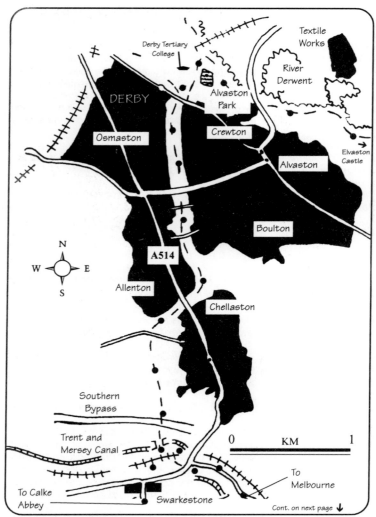

railway bridge, and onto a cycle path which crosses the canal and then the River Trent. Shortly after crossing the river, branch **R** off the cycle path, uphill to a T-junction and **R** into King's Newton. Go straight across the road by the market cross and emerge in Melbourne by a new housing estate. Go **L** then immediate **R** onto the main road. Take the first **L** signed for Wilson / Breedon

Cont. on next page ↓

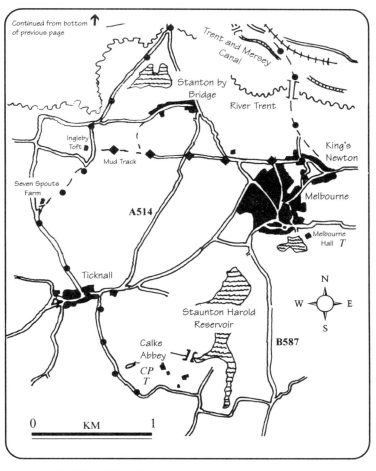

Continued from bottom of previous page ↑

Trent and Mersey Canal

Stanton by Bridge

River Trent

King's Newton

Melbourne

Ingleby Toft

Mud Track

Seven Spouts Farm

A514

Melbourne Hall *T*

Ticknall

Staunton Harold Reservoir

B587

N
W   E
S

Calke Abbey
CP
T

0   KM   1

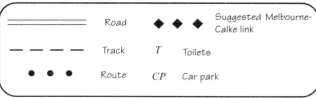

─────	Road	◆ ◆ ◆	Suggested Melbourne-Calke link
── ── ──	Track	*T*	Toilets
• • •	Route	*CP*	Car park

then bear **L** again by the White Swan pub to emerge opposite Melbourne Hall.

d. SWARKESTONE LOCK-CALKE ABBEY

At Swarkestone Lock carry straight on over the canal bridge and down the rough track to emerge at the main road. Cross straight over and pass through the village to meet the A514 and go **R** . Take the first **R** immediately over the bridge signed for Ingleby. Take the second **L** and in about 3/4 of a mile the road hairpins to the right, uphill. Head **L** off the road here (actually following the line of the road straight on) through a gate and onto a narrow track, with a dense wood on your left. Ignore any tracks off to the left and at the next farm bend left up the tarmac drive and exit at the first right hand bend to meet the road. Turn **L** onto this road and in a mile or so come into Ticknall. Head **L** on the A514 and **R** into Calke Abbey grounds. **Note:** a suggested link between Melbourne and Calke Abbey is shown on the map if you wish to visit both in the same trip.

ALONG THE WAY

Although the Derby-Melbourne cycle track passes through some suburbs it also has some fine country sections, in particular the stretch before Swarkestone Lock which follows the tree-lined course of the former **Derby Canal**. *This has now all but disappeared but originally joined the Trent and Mersey at Swarkestone Lock (for details of the latter canal see route 12).* **Melbourne Hall** *has a fine prospect over a lake and its twenty acres of grounds to the south are well worth exploring on foot. The hall was home to former Prime Ministers Lords Melbourne and Palmerston but is now open only in August (2pm-5pm), excluding the first three Mondays. The* **gardens** *are open on a more regular basis and were begun as early as 1700. Look out for the bird cage-shaped pergola. Entry fees for hall and garden. The nearby* **parish church** *has a magnificent interior.*

Calke Abbey *is one of the National Trust's most unusual properties. Home of the Harpur-Crewes, the house has been inhabited by several eccentric members of the family and is left virtually unchanged since the National Trust's acquisition of it. There are extensive personal collections of natural history and personal memorabilia reflecting the interests and personalities of various family members, much left as it was found, piled on beds for example. An oriental style eighteenth century state bed was found in its original packing cases and is now magnificently displayed. You can explore the grounds on foot and discover the church, the orangery, walled garden and deer park.*

14. ELVASTON CASTLE TO DERBY CENTRE

LENGTH AND DIFFICULTY *18km / 11 miles for a return trip into Derby and a circuit of the Elvaston Bridleway. This route is almost entirely off-road and mainly flat. The bridleway around Elvaston is shared in a few places by cars accessing the grounds (usually going very slowly). Remember to take a lock to secure your bike in Derby centre. The riverside path is a well made tarmac or hardpacked surface.*

MAPS *OS Landrangers 128 and 129, Derby and Nottingham respectively.*

TIME ESTIMATE *2-3 hours plus time to visit Elvaston Castle and Derby (lots to see).*

FACILITIES

Information *Offices at Elvaston Castle 01332 571342 and in Derby town centre 01332 255802.*

Eating *There is a cafe by the castle at Elvaston and plenty of places in Derby centre.*

BIKE ACCESS POINTS *Elvaston Castle is about 8km / 5 miles southeast of Derby centre, just off the A6 Loughborough road. The main car park at Elvaston Castle is signed off the B5010 just after passing through the village of Elvaston. This avoids the parking difficulties of starting in Derby centre. The trail is accessible for most of its length through the town centre and at:*

Alvaston Park
Raynesway (A5111)
Alvaston suburb (Green Lane)

ALONG THE WAY

*Both **Elvaston Castle Country Park** and **Derby city centre** have numerous attractions. Although there are many works alongside the River Derwent, which you follow between Elvaston and Derby, it provides a pleasant green corridor full of wildlife. Simply follow the riverside path into Derby until you meet the industrial museum. There are also pleasant green stretches such as Bass's Recreation Ground and Alvaston Park. A much better way to approach Derby than by car! Beware with children - some road crossings.*

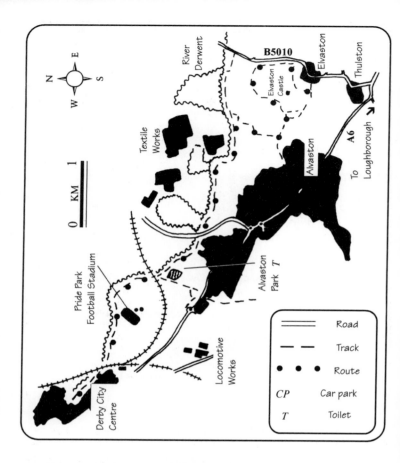

ELVASTON CASTLE COUNTRY PARK (see page 61 map)

1. ELVASTON CASTLE In fact not a castle but the former castellated stately home of the Stanhope family (Earls of Harrington). Built in 1817, it is surrounded by the Estate Museum (open April 1st - October 31st), information office and gift shop, cafe and countryside rangers' office.

2. CHURCH Contains several monuments to the Stanhope family, in particular one that records the achievements of the fifth Earl whilst in Greece with Byron.

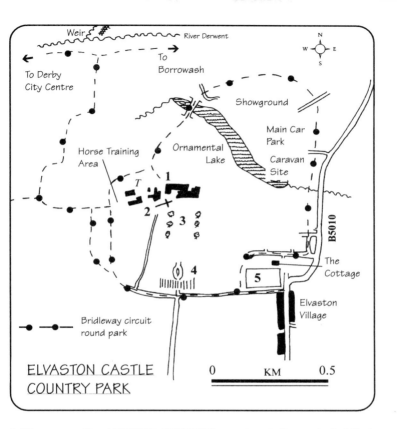

3. These magnificent FORMAL GARDENS were largely the product of Scot, William Barron's mind. He was responsible for such features as the 'Crown Bush' (obvious when you see it) and for the magnificent topiary here in general.

4. The GOLDEN GATES were probably originally at Versailles but came to Elvaston in 1819. They stand at the end of a half mile long avenue that leads down to the London Road and London Road Lodge.

5. The OLD ENGLISH GARDENS are walled and house a huge variety of plants and shrubs.

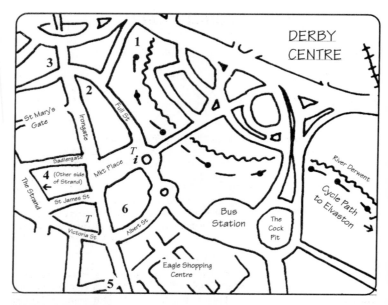

DERBY
CENTRE

DERBY CITY CENTRE ATTRACTIONS (Details of many others from Tourist Information)

1. INDUSTRIAL MUSEUM Conveniently next to the riverside cycle way and a good place to stop and explore the rest of Derby from. Houses a unique display of Rolls Royce engines including a Tristar engine which occupies a space equivalent to about half a semi-detached house! Upstairs is an impressive railway display and information about traditional industries.

2. DERBY CATHEDRAL Contains a beautifully unusual iron chancel screen as well as Bess of Hardwick's monument (see ride 18). The 212ft high tower is one of the tallest in England.

3. MONTAGE PHOTO GALLERY Exhibitions of contemporary photography.

4. MUSEUM AND ART GALLERY Local and natural history collections as one would expect plus an exhibition of the amazing works of local painter Joseph Wright and an orrery (clockwork model of the solar system).

5. DERBY HERITAGE CENTRE Changing displays on Derby's history.

6. VICTORIAN MARKET HALL

15. LONGENDALE

START *Torside Car Park*   **GRID REF** *067 984*

LENGTH *10km / 6 miles*   **TIME ESTIMATE** *1-2 hours*

MAPS *OS Outdoor Leisure 1, Dark Peak. Landranger 110, Sheffield and Huddersfield.*

SERVICES *Sizeable car park, toilets and (usually) snack van at your start point. No others along the way. Crowden Youth Hostel lies north of Torside Reservoir (see map). Tourist Information Office at Glossop 01457 855920.*

ROADS AND TRACKS *Virtually all off-road. Part of the route follows the excellent and easy Longendale Trail, a flat off-road path along a former railway line - see ride 1 for further details. The rest of the route follows tracks surrounding the reservoirs. Whilst the quality of the other tracks isn't up to the high standard of the trail they are still wide vehicle tracks. There is the odd gradient but this is a largely flat route.*

Leave Torside car park, heading away from the road and bend left away from the information point and toilets up a sandy track to meet the signed Longendale Trail. Go **R** onto the flat sandy trail as the steep, impressive bank of Torside Clough beneath Clough Edge towers up to your left. Soon you will meet the B6105 road. Go straight across and head **L** at the immediate split (right descends to cross the dam between Torside and Rhodeswood reservoirs).

Shortly a dark stone bridge appears, crossing over the trail, in front of you. About 100m before this head through the bridleway gate on your **R**, waymarked with bridleway and footpath arrows, to descend a steep sandy track to a road. Cross straight over the road and continue descending steeply (**beware of a small, steep ravine on the right here; dismount advisable**). The rocky track rises after bending left to improve gradually in quality as it runs alongside Valehouse Reservoir on the right. Join the tarmac at the end and bend 90 degrees right running over the dam wall between Valehouse and Bottom reservoirs. At the far side of the dam wall go 90 degrees right to pass through gates (marked as a private road) by a solid looking water board edifice. You are now riding along the northern bank of Valehouse reservoir, gloriously flanked by deciduous trees.

At the end of the reservoir zig-zag up the tarmac road to a T-junction with the road. On your right the road leads over the dam between Valehouse and Rhodeswood reservoirs. Bear **L** here, away from the dam, and immediately over a small bridge go **R** through a bridleway gate onto a rough track. Follow this track above Rhodeswood reservoir on the right, as high up on your left, above the forestry plantation, are the remains of a disused quarry. At the end of the track go through a bridleway gate to meet a tarmac road on a hairpin and **R** onto the road. Cross on the dam between Torside and Rhodeswood reservoirs and bear left at the end to meet the B6105 again. Cross over and rejoin the Longendale Trail to get back to Torside car park.

ALONG THE WAY

*The **reservoirs** were built in the mid-nineteenth century to fulfill the demand for clean water in Manchester, whose population had exploded during the Industrial Revolution. Such a water supply was needed to prevent health problems such as cholera in the overcrowded city.*

*__Glossop,__ only 6 or 7 km from the Torside car park, is an interesting town that, along with numerous others, proclaims itself to be a 'gateway to the Peak District'. Much of the town is Victorian whilst the conservation area of Old Glossop houses some lovely 17th century cottages. There is a **Heritage Centre** tracing the history of the town as well as a good assortment of cafes and pubs.*

FOR A MAP OF THE ROUTE SEE THE MAP ACCOMPANYING RIDE 1.

CALKE ABBEY (ROUTE 13)

16. DERWENT RESERVOIR

START *Fairholmes car park and information*   **GRID REF** *173 894*
centre between Ladybower and Derwent
Reservoirs.

LENGTH *17km / 10.5 miles*   **TIME ESTIMATE** *3 hours*

MAPS *OS Outdoor Leisure 1, Dark Peak. Landranger 110, Sheffield and Huddersfield.*

SERVICES *Toilets, cafe, Peak Park information office and cycle hire at the Fairholmes car park. The cycle hire centre has many bikes modified to carry younger children. Ring 01433 651261 for more details.*

ROADS AND TRACKS *Mainly off-road, although there is a lengthy section of minor road at the start of the route. This is closed to motor traffic at peak weekend times (every Sunday and Saturdays and Bank Holidays from Easter to the end of October) when you can complete a car-free ride.*

From the car park exit onto the road on the west side of Derwent Reservoir. Head north on the road, through the roundabout by the car park (up the road by signs indicating no access for motor vehicles on weekends and bank holidays). Simply follow this road until it ends towards the northern end of Howden Reservoir where, through a bridleway gate, it becomes a track. On the way you pass through Birchinlee plantation where you can see information boards describing the former village here (see Along the Way).

Carrying on along the track go through the plantation (much thinned at the time of writing) and split **R** at the only minor junction before coming to the beautiful Slippery Stones Bridge, formerly of Derwent village (see Along the Way). Over the bridge follow the bridleway sign **L**, shortly coming to a T-junction. From here there is a lovely prospect up the valley ahead of you to such wild moorland features as Crow Stones Edge. Go **R** here to follow the footpath sign for Derwent Valley (left up the valley leads to Langsett and Flouch Inn).

After a short climb up a stony track the gradient becomes mush easier as the surface improves. Look out for the unusual natural stone projections just underneath Long Edge, up to your left. After this taste of the wild country you reapproach civilisation and can glimpse the dramatic front wall of Howden Dam through the trees. Simply follow this steadily improving track until it meets a tarmac road (**beware some traffic**). **R** here leads you in front of Derwent Dam and back to Fairholmes.

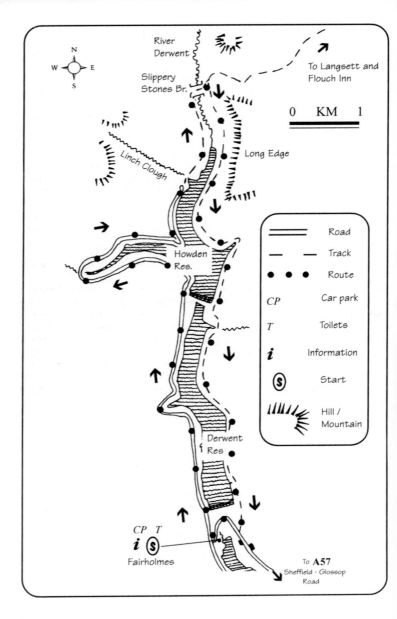

River
Derwent

To Langsett and
Flouch Inn

Slippery
Stones Br.

Long Edge

Linch Clough

0   KM   1

Howden
Res.

	Road
- - -	Track
• • •	Route
CP	Car park
T	Toilets
i	Information
Ⓢ	Start
⅏	Hill / Mountain

Derwent
Res

CP T
i Ⓢ
Fairholmes

To A57
Sheffield - Glossop
Road

N
W   E
S

ALONG THE WAY

The Derwent and Howden Reservoirs have flooded what was once a narrow valley, whilst commercial forestry covers many of the surrounding slopes; man's influence on the landscape is very evident hereabouts. However, the lonely moors, glimpsed as you round the northern end of the Howden Reservoir, have barely changed since medieval times when most of the deforestation in the area took place. They are most beautiful in early autumn when huge carpets of purple flowering heather present a colourful mosaic.

The former 'tin town' of **Birchinlee** has all but disappeared but note the information boards and the solitary brick furnace as you pass through the site of this settlement on the western side of the Howden dam. It once housed the workforce of navvies who constructed this huge engineering work over a period of fifteen years. The self- contained community had all its requirements provided within the village, including a canteen (pub) and a police station! A railway line was specially constructed to carry quarried stone for the dam into the valley from Grindleton.

The 'lost villages' of **Ashopton** and **Derwent** became so because of the completion of a third dam, Ladybower, opened in 1945. Although drowned by the new reservoir the villages' sad remains can be seen in times of drought (certainly visible in 1995/6). Slippery Stones Bridge, crossed at the end of the outward northern leg of the ride, was formerly the packhorse bridge near a splendid Jacobean hall in Derwent. A figure from the hall, 'Peeping Tom' is now in the visitor centre at Fairholmes. Even the dead villagers were reinterred in Bamford churchyard and the war memorial was also moved. However many fine buildings could not be saved; Ashopton Methodist chapel was one of the finest in the Peak area. The dams were important training grounds for the famous **'Dam Busters'** who dropped the 'bouncing bomb' on the Ruhr valley in World War II.

17. SHIPLEY COUNTRY PARK

START *The country park can be accessed*   **GRID REF** *431 452*
from a number of points by car and by bike
(see map for details).

LENGTH AND TIME *Use the scale map opposite to plan your own route. There are numerous miles of good bridleway track throughout the country park. You can spend an hour or most of the day exploring the tracks and park attractions.*

MAPS *OS Landranger 129, Nottingham, doesn't have much detail of the park on but is OK for general location. Otherwise use the map opposite.*

SERVICES *Cycle hire and information by the visitor centre as marked on the map 01773 719961. Includes tandems and cycles for the disabled. There is a cafe at the visitor centre.*

ROADS AND TRACKS *Excellent off-road bridleway network and some on-road sections (slow traffic). The centre of the park is on a slight hill and some of the tracks can become a little muddy when wet but generally speaking the park is excellent for all bikers except the most absolute beginners, with most tracks not being shared with motor traffic.*

ALONG THE WAY

*Shipley Country Park was the estate of the **Miller-Mundy nobles** in the eighteenth century. As well as being their country home with surrounding grounds, the underground coal reserves were also exploited by the family. In 1922 the land passed to the Shipley Colliery Company which became part of the NCB in 1947. The grounds were acquired by the County Council and in 1976 became a public park. There was once a fine hall at the centre of the park but this was demolished during WWII. However, several fine **lodges and cottages** can be seen about the park. The network of bridleways and paths are based on a series of railway lines on the estate that were used to transport the coal. Links with the Nutbrook Trail, current and planned, are discussed in ride 11. There are plenty of family and fitness activities in the park including a trim track, toddlers' play area, day ticket fishing, wayfaring and birdwatching. The theme park **The American Adventure** lies at the centre of the park although it is under separate ownership.*

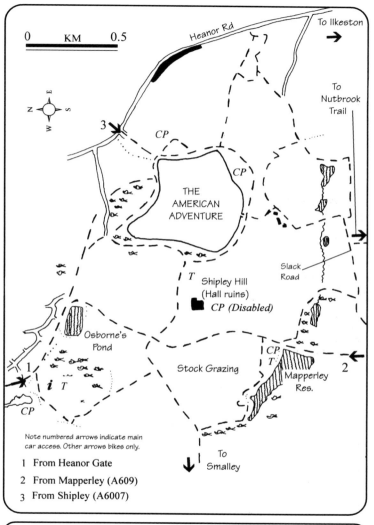

The map shows The American Adventure theme park area.

- **Heanor Rd** — road along the top of the map
- **To Ilkeston** (arrow, top right)
- **To Nutbrook Trail** (right side)
- **0 KM 0.5** (scale bar)
- Compass rose (N, E, S, W)
- **3** (arrow) CP
- CP
- **THE AMERICAN ADVENTURE**
- **Slack Road**
- **T Shipley Hill (Hall ruins)**
- **CP (Disabled)**
- **Osborne's Pond**
- **1** (arrow) *i* **T**
- **CP**
- **Stock Grazing**
- **CP T Mapperley Res.**
- **2** (arrow)
- **To Smalley** (arrow, bottom)

Note numbered arrows indicate main car access. Other arrows bikes only.

1 From Heanor Gate
2 From Mapperley (A609)
3 From Shipley (A6007)

– – – – –	Bridleway for cyclists	*T* Toilets
CP	Car park	*i* Visitor centre and cafe

69

18. HARDWICK HALL

START *Hardwick Hall Country Park car park*   **GRID REF** *453 640*
(small charge made). Open daylight hours.

LENGTH *14km / 8.7 miles*   **TIME ESTIMATE** *3-3.5 hours plus*
                                           visiting time for Hardwick Hall.

MAPS *OS Landranger 120, Mansfield and Worksop.*

SERVICES *There is a restaurant at Hardwick Hall (see opening hours below),*
a pub in Fackley and another at the end of your journey, near Hardwick Hall.

ROADS AND TRACKS *A grassy bridleway, good track and former railway line*
on the Pleasley Trails network are mixed in with minor roads. The initial climb
in the grounds of Hardwick Hall is worth the effort for the spectacular view of
the buildings. From then on gradients are easy.

With the information centre at Hardwick Hall car park on your right, head away
from it to cross a small bridge and follow a wide dirt track. Immediately after
passing quarry workings on the left take a **L** on a marked bridlepath which
takes you into a large field. The narrow tread of the path is obvious as it climbs
towards the crest of the hill with inspiring views of Hardwick Hall on the right.
Through a small group of trees you meet a tarmac road. You can visit Hardwick
Hall by going right here. Retrace your steps back to this point **but wheel your
bike when returning**- the road is one way. The line of the bridleway continues
over the road. Wooden posts guide you over the brow to a large wooden gate
by a fine residence with a 1724 datestone. Through the gate continue on the
track into the quiet village of Ault Hucknall.

At the T-junction with the minor road in Ault Hucknall go **R**, passing the fine
Parish Church of John the Baptist on the left. Out of the village take the first **R**
and follow the road into Rowthorne. Just as you enter the village go **R** onto a
minor road which heads towards a spoil heap near Pleasley. The road then
descends through woods and passes under a bridge. Very shortly after this the
Teversal Trail crosses the road; pick it up on the **R**. Follow the trail for about a
kilometre until another trail joins obliquely from the right, marked to Teversal
Visitor Centre. Follow this leafy trail past the visitor centre on the left and straight
over a junction to descend to a road in Teversal. Go **L** here and **R** at the next
junction to pass through Fackley. This minor road brings you to a junction in
Stanley and a **R** turn brings Hardwick Hall back into view. After another kilometre
you pass a car park and a minor road leading to the Hardwick Inn on the right.
At the next split bear right, following signs for Stainsby and Heath to bring you
back to the entrance to Hardwick Hall Country Park car park.

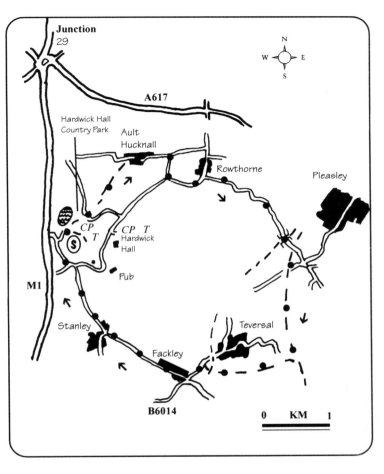

ALONG THE WAY

Hardwick Hall is a superb Elizabethan mansion owned by the National Trust. Its beautiful facade gave rise to the saying 'Hardwick Hall, more glass than wall'. The huge ES initials on the towers are those of the hall's creator, Elizabeth, Countess of Shrewsbury. Known as Bess of Hardwick, she had a formidable reputation, based partly on her ability to marry wealthy and powerful husbands. Open: 26th March - 2nd December. Hall and Shop Weds, Thurs, Sat, Sun and Bank Holiday Mondays, 12.30 - 5.00 pm. Restaurant open same days as hall from 2.00 pm. Gardens open daily from noon - 5.30 pm. Admission charge.

The **Teversal Trail** is part of the Pleasley Trails network, based on old rail tracks laid to exploit the local coal reserves. The tracks were closed in a piece-meal fashion throughout the twentieth century. (See route 7).

HARDWICK HALL (ROUTE 18)

19. CARSINGTON RESERVOIR

START *Carsington Water visitor centre car park*   **GRID REF** *242 517*

LENGTH *14km / 8.5 miles*   **TIME ESTIMATE** *2-3 hours*

MAPS *OS Landranger 119, Buxton and Matlock.*

SERVICES *Large pay and display car park, visitor centre with coffee shop, children's play area, toilets and telephones, together at start. Cycle hire is also available from near the visitor centre. Bookings and enquiries 01629 540478. There are car parks at Millfields and Sheepwash, the former with toilets.*

ROADS AND TRACKS *The minor road through Hopton and Carsington is quite fast though easily 'pushable.' The rest of the ride is off-road on undulating track. This is definitely the hardest of the 'easy' circular routes.*

The cycle trail lies behind the main visitor centre car park. From the car park join the track and head **L** on it, towards the sailing club, in a southerly direction. Shortly after crossing a road follow the blue horse and cycle signs up the right. This diverts you from the footpath round the edge of the dam and drops down beneath the southwestern edge of the reservoir. As on the rest of the route follow advisory signs and you should climb back up to cross over the road and bear **R** onto the trail. Just after passing the entrance to the Millfield site, which you see signed, pick up the **L** onto a track, waymarked with the usual blue signs.

Pass behind Millfields. After several small drops and rises meet a T-junction and bear **L** down the unmarked track (right may be marked Herbs/Alpines/200yds). You now begin to follow signs for Hopton village, passing by Upperfields Farm. The cycle route is now clearly marked until it reaches the main road before Hopton. Any possible wrong turnings are clearly marked as private. Crossing over the main road you come to the village of Hopton and bear **L** onto the road which takes you through the village and into Carsington. Simply follow the road until you meet the main road again and go more or less straight across, following the sign for the Sheepwash car park. Follow the main track and the cycle and horse markers to bring you back to the main car park area by the visitor centre.

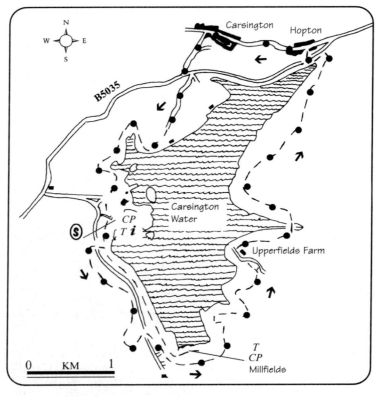

═══════	Road	*CP* Car park	*i* Information
─ ─ ─ ─	Track	*T* Toilets	⑃ Hill / Mountain
●●●	Route	Ⓢ Start	

ALONG THE WAY

Carsington Reservoir *was purposely designed with family tourism in mind. It features Stones island with its interactive hill top monument and ideal picnic location, the Kugel (a large granite sphere suspended by water), a water sports centre and bird hide, on top of the basic facilities listed in the introductory details. The reservoir itself supplies water for three million people in Derbyshire,*

Nottinghamshire and Leicestershire. Most of the water here is collected from the River Derwent when its level is high.

Hopton *village houses some delightful buildings, most notably the almshouses and Hopton Hall. The former bear an inscription telling us the 'hospital' was left for the benefit of two poor men and two poor women. The latter is seen passing out of Hopton and is largely Elizabethan though partly altered in the 1700s. Note the beautiful curves of the brick boundary wall.* **Carsington** *village has the Church of St. Margaret (a 1648 Gothic style edifice).*

THE HIGH PEAK TRAIL (ROUTE 8)

20. EYAM

START *Eyam village car park, opposite museum.*   **GRID REF** *216 767*

LENGTH *12km / 7.5miles*   **TIME ESTIMATE** *2-3 hours*

MAPS *OS Outdoor Leisure 24, White Peak. Landranger 119, Buxton and Matlock.*

SERVICES *There are two car parks in Eyam (one for visitors to Eyam Hall only, the other pay and display) plus toilets, and a general grocers. If visiting Eyam Hall you can get refreshments at their cafe. Great Hucklow and Foolow each have a pub.*

ROADS AND TRACKS *Mainly on minor roads. Once over the initial steep gradient you follow minor roads but beware of the traffic through Eyam and Foolow.*

From the car park opposite Eyam museum turn **R** and climb steeply up the hill for about 1km, passing Eyam Youth Hostel on the way. As the climb begins to level out take the first **L** signed for Bretton, Great Hucklow and Abney. The road levels out now all the hard work is done and gives you great views over Eyam to the quarries on the other side of Middleton Dale. Pass the Barrel Inn at Bretton and take the next turning **R**, ignoring the road straight on signed for Foolow. There are great views to your left over Stanley Moor as you ride onto Hucklow Edge. Ignore the next right for the gliding club and Abney but take the next **L** after a lengthy descent, signed for Grindlow (you can also explore Great Hucklow which is straight on here). Keeping on the same road through the hamlet of Grindlow you eventually meet a busier road where you have two options:

OPTION 1: Go **L** on this fast road to bring you into Foolow.
OPTION 2: Cross straight over the road and down the gravel driveway, picking up the single width track to the left of the bungalow. Follow the narrow track down Silly Dale to come to a T-junction with a walled grass track which you bear **L** onto. This can be difficult and overgrown but persevere and you will soon come to the road. Go **R** into Foolow.

Once in Foolow take the **R** by the telephone box opposite the pub and signed for Wardlow and Middleton. In Housley ignore the right turn for Wardlow. Immediately before the junction with the main A623 look for a rough track on your **L**, signed "unsuitable for motor vehicles." At its beginning it is slightly hilly and muddy but its surface gradually improves and eventually it becomes metalled and leads into the back of Eyam to join the main road. Go **R** here back into the village and then **L** back to the car park.

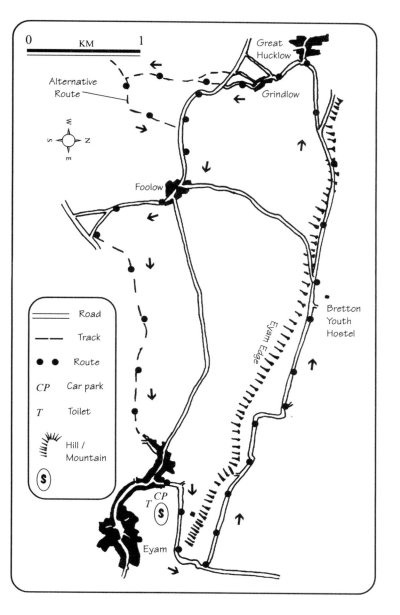

ALONG THE WAY

Eyam's most famous claim to fame, and one you cannot miss on a walk through the village, where it is described on detailed plaques, is that it was decimated by The Plague in 1665-6. It arrived in the form of fleas carried in a box of cloth from London by a tailor. The local ministers imposed a year long curfew on the village in order to contain the dreadful disease. Food was left for the villagers at various points round the village and money was left in return. 259 people died out of a village population of 350. The 13th century St. Lawrence's church contains a number of unusual relics. Mompesson's Chair (named after the local rector) dates from 1665 and there is also the plague register and a cupboard made from the wood of the box that brought The Plague to Eyam. Outside stands the best example of a Saxon cross in the whole of Derbyshire. Also look out for the unusual headstone of Harry Bagshaw, the cricketer! **Eyam Hall** is a superb 17th century manor house. You must visit on a timed guided tour basis and should book in advance to make certain of a place. It also contains a buttery for refreshment. Opposite the hall look out for the old market hall and the stocks used by the Barmote Court for the punishment of lead miners. **Eyam Museum** is opposite your start point and centres around the story of how the plague reached Eyam. It also contains geological and heritage displays. The centre of **Foolow** is dominated by the small pond on the green and a medieval cross. The latter still has a ring attached to it that was used for bull baiting; dogs taunted the bull in the belief that it would tenderise the meat. There is also a small church and manor house.

ELVASTON CASTLE (ROUTES 13 AND 14)

21. CHELMORTON

START *Chelmorton village*   **GRID REF** *114 701*

LENGTH *14km / 8.7miles*   **TIME ESTIMATE** *3 hours*

MAPS *OS Outdoor Leisure 24, The White Peak. Landranger 119, Buxton and Matlock.*

SERVICES *Roadside parking in Chelmorton which has a small post office and a pub. Flagg has a pub, accommodation in the form of a pub B&B and a caravan site. There is also a pub at Pomeroy.*

ROADS AND TRACKS *Mainly quiet minor roads, some barely used at all. One short stretch of busy main road and an option to use a short section of tricky green lane.*

In Chelmorton climb gently up the main street, away from the Methodist church and towards the spire of the Church of St. John the Baptist. (See Along the Way). You can visit the latter by going straight on at the dead end sign at the end of the main street (the village pub is found opposite the church). To continue on the route bear **R** just before the dead end sign, onto Church Lane. At the next junction head **L** for Flagg and Taddington. Shortly take the next **L** signed for Taddington and head gently uphill on this more minor road. Ignore the next left and the next right as you head across Taddington Moor. Take the next unsigned **R,** a very minor road. Coming to the T-junction with a more major road **(look out for potholes)** go **R** and head downhill for about 1.5km to a crossroads. Head straight across here, signed for Flagg and Monyash. Ignore left turns to continue into the old lead mining settlement of Flagg.

In Flagg ignore the left turn and carry on along the road to pass a small church. Proceed uphill to the next very minor, unmarked **L** (easy to miss), immediately passing Town Head Farm on the right. At the next junction you are faced with a three way split; take the right-hand most option which is the most minor of the three options. Follow this to the A515 and go **R (CAUTION - VERY BUSY ROAD -** pushing on the verge may be advisable). Pass through Pomeroy, a collection of a few houses and the Duke of York pub, and shortly take the next **R** (easy to miss as it isn't signed from the main road). You soon come to a fork and have two options to conclude your route;

OPTION 1. Carry straight on, on the unmarked track to follow this old green lane between walls. Can be muddy in winter. Emerging at the road go **L** then **R** to retrace your steps back into Chelmorton.

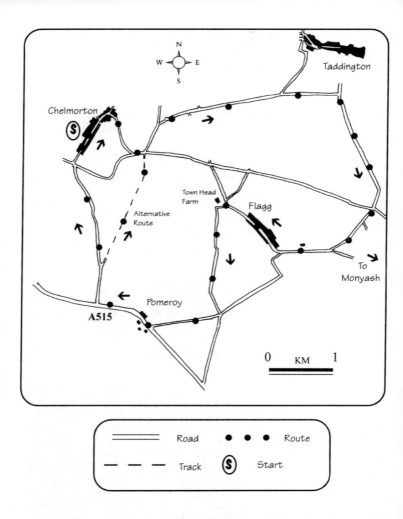

OPTION 2. Ignore the track which goes straight on and simply stay on the road and follow it downhill which reveals a great view of Chelmorton beneath you. Go across the next crossroads and back into the village centre.

ALONG THE WAY

Perhaps the most notable feature of **Chelmorton** is the pattern of **dry stone walls** surrounding the village. The immediate area has, supposedly, the highest concentration of these beautiful landscape features in the whole of the country, due in part to the fact that there are some farms in the village that still maintain the medieval strip field system. The **Church of St. John the Baptist** can boast that, at 1200ft, it is the highest in Derbyshire. The entrance contains unusual coffins showing the trades of the deceased including forester, depicted by a horn, axe and arrow. Unusually the weathercock is in the shape of a locust as St. John is said to have survived in the wilderness on locusts and honey. Although the setting of the old lead mining settlement of **Flagg** may not rival that of Chelmorton it has some interesting buildings. **Flagg Hall**, an Elizabethan edifice, is the main point of interest although, not open to the public. A skull has lain within the house for some centuries and it is said if it is removed extreme bad luck will occur.

TYPICAL WHITE PEAK SCENERY NEAR CHELMORTON (ROUTE 21)

22. PARWICH

START *Tissington Trail - Alsop Station*   **GRID REF** *157 547*
               car park (pay and display)

LENGTH *17km / 10.5 miles*   **TIME ESTIMATE** *3-4 hours*

MAPS *OS Outdoor Leisure 24, The White Peak. Landranger 119, Buxton and Matlock.*

SERVICES *Pay and display car park and picnic site only, at Alsop Station. Village shop, pub and telephone in Parwich.*

ROADS AND TRACKS *A real mix; the excellently surfaced Tissington Trail combines with a green lane (muddy in winter), minor roads and a very small section of 'A' road. This quiet route aims to get you away from such tourist 'honeypots' as Dovedale.*

From Alsop Station car park head **L** onto the trail and immediately pass back under the A515. Simply stay on this trail, with good initial views to the left, as the sloping green landscape slips away into Wolfscote Dale, backed by limestone knolls. About 5km after the start, and after passing over and under several bridges, turn off the trail as you cross the road at Biggin (in fact your first opportunity to exit the trail - just over the bridge at Biggin look for a track down to the road on your right). On meeting the road go **L** uphill, heading away from the village. At the main A515 (**CAUTION VERY BUSY**) turn **R** then immediate **L** to head down an unmarked, rough track (very muddy in winter). Ignore the first opportunity to turn left and carry on through the gate. The track becomes a difficult green lane. Follow it in a straight line as it goes through a field and pick up the green lane at the other side (look out for Minninglow Hill ahead with its tumuli). Join a T-junction with a green lane and bear **L**. This becomes a reasonable vehicle track and passes The Nook to come to a crossroads. Go **R** onto the minor road and bear **R** at the first split after about 2km. Eventually you come to a T-junction (**BEWARE - STEEP DESCENT AND SHARP BEND BEFOREHAND**). Turn **L** into Parwich. Look out for the brick facade of Parwich Hall on the left, ignoring the left split by the hall. Go **R** in front of the village shop (although it's worth going straight on for a look at the church). Past the school take the **R** handmost option, "unsuitable for motors." Climb and drop steeply on this tiny village road to come to a T-junction. Go **R** and head away from the village on this undulating road to come into Alsop en le Dale. Carry on until you join the main A515 (**BEWARE, BUSY**) and go **L**. Your start point soon appears on your **L,** signed Alsop Station, after a couple of minutes on the A road.

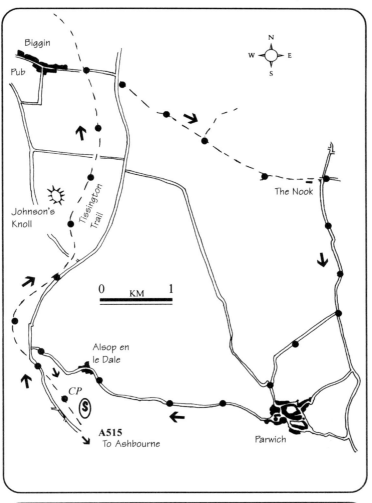

Biggin

Pub

Johnson's
Knoll

Tissington Trail

The Nook

0   KM   1

Alsop en
le Dale

CP

A515
To Ashbourne

Parwich

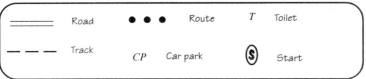

——— Road	● ● ● Route	*T* Toilet
– – – Track	*CP* Car park	Ⓢ Start

ALONG THE WAY

Parwich is an interesting stop, with its grand, brick-facaded Georgian hall and late 19th century church. The hall was rebuilt in 1747 though parts dating from the 16th century original were incorporated. Similarly the Church of St.Peter incorporates a Norman tympanum over the door, bearing the Lamb of God, a pig, two snakes, a stag, a horse and a bird.

PARWICH HALL (ROUTE 22)

23. BRADWELL

START *Bradwell village centre*   **GRID REF** *174 811*

LENGTH *15km / 9.3 miles*   **TIME ESTIMATE** *3 hours*

MAPS *OS Outdoor Leisure Maps 1 and 24, Dark and White Peak respectively. Landranger 110, Sheffield / Huddersfield. (Small part of route on 119, Buxton and Matlock).*

SERVICES *On-road parking, toilets and variety of shops in Bradwell which also features the sixteenth century Old Bowling Green Inn.*

ROADS AND TRACKS *A mix of minor roads and off road tracks (mainly well-surfaced but a final rocky descent). There is also a small section of busy road. Some fairly steep gradients mean riders should have some experience.*

From the centre of Bradwell follow the main road, the B6049, back to the small settlement of Brough, 2.5km to the north.(**TAKE CARE; FAST MAIN ROAD - PUSHING BIKES ON THE PAVEMENT IS ADVISABLE).** Take the first minor turning on the **R** up Brough Lane, signed as a dead end for cars. After a steepish climb ignore the road as it hairpins to the right and carry straight on, leaving the road and going through a gate onto a well-surfaced track. Behind you Lose Hill rises up. Follow the track as it climbs steeply and after levelling out it passes a track on the right. Simply follow the main track until it passes through a gate to meet a tarmac road. This becomes a delightful country lane (Townfield Lane) and leads to Shatton. At the T-junction in the small village of Shatton go **L** and very shortly, at the first fork by a white house on the right (Brookside) bear **R.**

Follow this road for a kilometre or so, passing the track up to Westfield and Peppercorn Houses, and come to a split. A sign indicates to the right a private way leads to Garner House; carry straight on marked for Offerton with a yellow arrow. Part of the section between Garner House and Offerton Hall can be muddy before you rejoin a good tarmac road. Stay on the road between several splendid buildings, climbing steeply. The more level section now gives you great views, on the left, of Stanage Edge and Hathersage some way beneath it. Descend over Dunge Brook and climb to a T-junction where you go **R.**

Passing Highlow Hall on the left there are good views towards Eyam Moor. Simply stay on this pleasant road for some 2.5km and enter the charming village of Abney. Just before the telephone box take a very minor, unmarked road to the **R.** Continue climbing to its terminus at a junction of tracks (note the unusually shaped hill of Abney Low behind you as you climb). A sign indicates

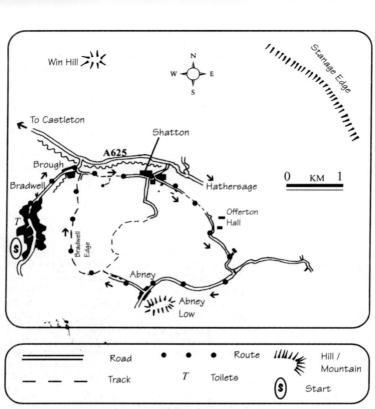

that you have come from Abney and that the right hand track is a public bridleroad to Shatton. Take the unsigned option to the **L** (you can take the bridleroad back to Shatton and retrace your original steps as another option). The track curves round to the right passing underneath the high ground of Bleak Knoll to the left. Great views open up to the right with the distinctive peaks of Win and Lose Hills in the distance. The track becomes increasingly rocky as you descend. Look out for a great view over the quarry between Bradwell and Castleton on the left before joining the tarmac road just past Elmore Hill Farm. Follow this road back into Brough to the main road and carefully retrace your steps back to Bradwell.

ALONG THE WAY

Although this is one of the hardest routes in the book it is worth pushing your bikes over the more difficult sections to attain superb views over the River Noe to the north. The most prominent peaks are **Lose Hill** *and* **Win Hill,** *both over 1500ft and supposedly reflecting a legendary military conflict in the area, losers and winners retreating to the respective summits.*

The road after Offerton Hall gives you a great opportunity to contemplate the straight gritstone horizon of **Stanage Edge** *to the north. This imposing feature is popular with climbers who you may be able to spot if you bring your binoculars along. The cement works between Bradwell, Hope and Castleton stands out like a sore thumb against the glorious backdrop of the Vale of Edale.*

CALTON PASTURES (ROUTE 24)

24. CHATSWORTH

START *Bakewell station (disused)*   **GRID REF** *222 691*
on the Monsal Trail

LENGTH *11km / 7miles*   **TIME ESTIMATE** *3-4 hours*

MAPS *OS Outdoor Leisure 24, The White Peak. Landranger 119, Buxton and Matlock.*

SERVICES *Free parking by Bakewell Station on the Monsal Trail. Toilets, tourist information and a wealth of cafes and pubs can be found in Bakewell. The trail is less than a kilometre from the centre of Bakewell up the quite steep Station Rd, found after crossing the River Wye on the right. Edensor has a cafe attached to the post office shop and a telephone box. Cafe and restaurant at Chatsworth.*

ROADS AND TRACKS *There is just about everything on this route, which makes it an ideal introduction to mountain biking proper. Steepish gradients, rocky paths, single width tracks and a small section of the Monsal Trail combine to make it an exciting and scenic ride for ambitious younger riders. The great views are well worth the effort of the hill climbs ! There is a very small section of main road, easily avoided.*

From the car park in front of Bakewell Station, on the Monsal Trail, take the road carried by a bridge over the Monsal Trail and begin to climb steeply. Simply stay on what becomes a minor road as it passes through woods and hairpins to reach the top of the hill. Over the brow, a good wide panorama stretches out in front of you, including gritstone edges over to your left, showing the close proximity of Dark and White Peak (see introduction for an explanantion). After less than a kilometre of descent head **R** off the road down a stony, tree-lined track and continue descending on it, in a more or less straight line, to arrive at the village of Edensor (see Along the Way). After a look around this fascinating village and church follow the main street to the main road and go **R (CAUTION - VERY FAST).**

Branch off the main road and effectively cut the corner off the right hand bend by following the wooden marker posts on the broad grassy area (the main entrance to Chatsworth is signposted off the road down to your left). Rejoin the main road and head uphill and very shortly look for the wooden marker post on the large grassy expanse to your **R**. Strike off towards it - the line of the bridleway here is very indistinct. It heads almost straight up the hill to a second marker post and then a clearer track leads you parallel to the wood edge, up to your left. After following parallel to the woods for some 300yds you come to a very large entrance gate to the woods by an information board detailing Chatsworth

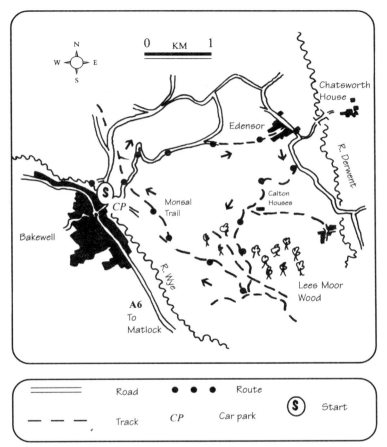

═══	Road	● ● ●	Route
— — —	Track	*CP*	Car park
		(S)	Start

Park. Go through the gate and climb through New Piece Wood, then follow straight over the middle of the next field, ignoring the footpath that leads off to the right. Drop down on the other side of the field following the wall on the left, to come to a bridleway marker indicating a split in front of you. Head off uphill again, to the **R,** following the edge of the plantation on your left. At the corner of the plantation the track leads you through a gap between two plantations. Follow the track, which becomes single width, over this very large field with great views behind you.

Meet the gate at the other side of the pasture and follow through two gates, picking up the waymarkers into the conifer plantation. Follow the waymarkers and this forest track and quite shortly a stunning view over Bakewell appears as you come to the brink of a steep hill. The track jinks left and quite steeply downhill here. The wide earth track comes to a T-junction with a bridleway marker directing you to the **L** (Haddon Estate to the right). At the next split follow the waymarker to the **R** and carry on downhill to a junction where you have three options. Take the **R** hand most option, marked in red (a byway) as going to Bakewell. The track steadily improves after a muddy section and passes through Coombs Farm. Nearly two kilometres after the last junction you meet Coombs Road viaduct. There is access onto the end of the Monsal Trail here which can then be followed back to Bakewell Station using a kilometre or so of the trail.

ALONG THE WAY

*The unusual architectural style of the village of **Edensor** reflects its creation. It was in the mid-nineteenth century that the then Duke of Devonshire decided that the current village of Edensor was spoiling the view from Chatsworth House, and so decided to move it lock, stock and barrel to Edensor's present location. When the architect called with the plans for the new village the Duke was so busy with another matter that he simply ordered one of each design for the village. Hence, amongst others, Georgian, Swiss and Italian styles are apparent in these beautifully preserved buildings. The village church was rebuilt in 1870 but retained many features of the original. The solemn and awe-inspiring monument to William and Henry Cavendish, sons of Bess of Hardwick, particularly stands out. Their effigies, one a skeleton and one shroud-clad lie austere and silent. There is also a wreath of everlasting flowers opposite the monument sent by Queen Victoria on the death of Lord Frederick Cavendish, murdered in 1912 by Sinn Fein.*

***Chatsworth House** will need no introduction to many. One of the north's most famous stately homes it is an ideal break from the ride and contains something for all ages. At the centre of the estate is the splendid Elizabethan mansion house, surrounded by a magnificent landscape, the design of Capability Brown. There are 100 acres of garden and several miles of walking within the grounds, including a maze and several cottage gardens. Of more interest to children, perhaps, are the farmyard and adventure playground.*

Charges for house and garden (lesser charges made for admission to component parts): Adults £6.75 Children £3.50 Family ticket £15.00 (saving if more than one child). For the latest opening details ring 01246 582204

If you plan to visit the house during the ride allow for a very full day !

NEAR CALTON HOUSES (ROUTE 24)

25. MACCLESFIELD FOREST

START *Car park opposite Trentabank Reservoir*   **GRID REF** *962 712*
in the Macclesfield Forest or other car parks marked
on the map.

LENGTH *8km / 5 miles*   **TIME ESTIMATE** *2-3 hours*
(harder option = 10km / 6.2km)

MAPS *OS Outdoor Leisure 24, White Peak. Landranger 118, Stoke on Trent and Macclesfield.*

SERVICES *There are information points at Trentabank Reservoir car park (which also has a ranger service) and Standing Stone car park. Refreshments at Leathers Smithy pub. Further pubs and telephones in nearby·Langley.*

ROADS AND TRACKS *Minor road and forest track. The harder option takes in a steep rocky track. A popular weekend and holiday spot so be aware of increased traffic at this time.*

Turn **L** out of the car park and shortly take the next **L**. Climb up this road and after coming over the crest of the hill go **L** onto a forest track, following the blue arrow. This track climbs quite steeply at the western edge of the forest with good views. Staying on the track, another prolonged climb brings you to a superb viewpoint with a bench on your left, with reservoirs in the valley bottom and hills rising to the north. Descend steeply to a T-junction and bear **R**, signposted for Shutlingsloe and Standing Stone. Stay on this track, ignoring any small turnings off to the right and emerge at a road junction. Go straight across here for Macclesfield Forest, passing Standing Stone car park and information point on the left. Take the next **L** signposted for Macclesfield Forest and Chapel. This superb road flattens out, then descends into the hamlet of Macclesfield Forest. At the junction in Macclesfield Forest stay on the road, bending left, signed Langley. This road takes you over Toot Hill.

Harder Option: In Macclesfield Forest you may want to choose the harder option. (Caution - very steep climb - a difficult push). Instead of bending left on the road take the stony track almost straight on which climbs steeply, signed with a white triangle no.3. Follow this to eventually emerge at a T-junction with a road and go **L**. After a short, steep descent bear **L** onto a forest track and follow yellow arrows and white bridleway signs for Langley at every opportunity to descend to the road. Go **R** onto the road. You have finished this more difficult option.

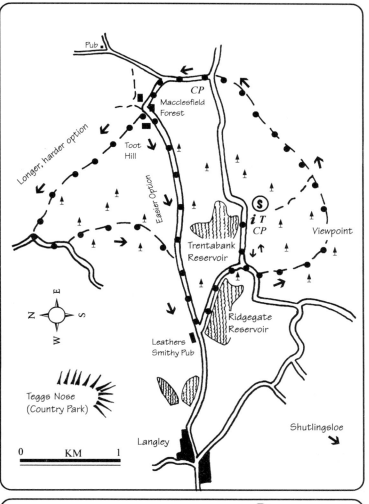

Pub

CP
Macclesfield
Forest

Longer, harder option

Toot
Hill

Easier Option

(S)
i T
CP

Viewpoint

Trentabank
Reservoir

Ridgegate
Reservoir

Leathers
Smithy Pub

N E S W

Teggs Nose
(Country Park)

Shutlingsloe

Langley

0   KM   1

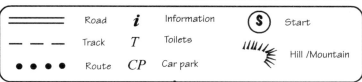

═══	Road	*i*	Information	(S) Start
– – –	Track	T	Toilets	
●●●●	Route	CP	Car park	⋰⋰ Hill /Mountain

Descend to the T-junction at Leathers Smithy pub and go **L**, passing Ridgegate Reservoir on your immediate right. Ignore the next right to stay on this road back to your starting point.

ALONG THE WAY

Macclesfield Forest was originally the name given to the extensive royal hunting forest in this area but today it usually refers to the forestry plantation where this ride is based. It is also the name of the delightful hamlet you pass through half way around the route, with its own tiny forest chapel. There is a herd of red deer here although they are very elusive. Depending on the time of year, various bird species inhabit the reservoirs, including grebes and ducks such as goldeneye, teal and pochard. **Shutlingsloe**, otherwise known as the Chesire Matterhorn, can be seen sticking its head above surrounding hills as you pass over Toot Hill. Although only 498m (1659 feet) in height it has a distinctly alpine appearance. There is also a superb view of **Tegg's Nose**, lying just outside the national park boundary, from the road descent on the harder option.

RESTING AT MACCLESFIELD FOREST VIEWPOINT (ROUTE 25)

CYCLING TITLES FROM EXCELLENT BOOKS

ULTIMATE GUIDES TO THE NATIONAL CYCLE NETWORK

C2C £6.95 ISBN 1-901464-02-4
Thames Valley £7.95 ISBN 1-901464-04-0
West Country Way £8.95 ISBN 1-901464-03-2
Devon C2C £5.95 ISBN 1-901464-06-7
Reivers (return C2C) £6.95 ISBN 1-901464-05-9
White Rose £6.95 ISBN 1-901464-08-3
Trans Pennine Trail Accommodation
& Visitor Guide £4.95 ISBN 1-901464-09-1

REGIONAL GUIDES

Yorkshire Dales Cycle Way £5.50 ISBN 1-870141-28-8
West Yorkshire Cycle Way £5.50 ISBN 1-870141-38-5
Biking Country Glasgow £5.99 ISBN 1-870141-45-8
Mountain Biking Eden Valley / N. Cumbria £5.95
ISBN 1-870141-07-5
Mountain Biking Lancs / S. Pennines £5.99
ISBN 1-901464-00-8

NEW OUT - MAY 2001

Cyclists' Route Handbook - North England
£9.95 ISBN 1-901464-10-5
All the major waymarked leisure routes in this area brought together for the first time in one book. Hundreds of photos, maps and factfiles make it an invaluable addition to any cyclist's bookshelf. Includes all long-distance routes plus traffic free trails and more than 100 suggested day rides. Full colour throughout.